"The true events Juan Ortiz relates in Never Forsaken have guided and inspired me for years. Juan's friendship, example, and influence have been invaluable in my life. Now, those same stories, their lessons and perspective, are available for you. Never Forsaken explains why the Ortiz family now lives as they do. More than that, it holds the answer to the life you desire for your family."

–Andy Andrews
New York Times bestselling author of
The Traveler's Gift & The Noticer

"A powerful example of the strength and resilience of the human spirit! Juan's story is a real life testament that it is not life's circumstances that determine your success but rather your response to those circumstances. Never Forsaken will inspire, encourage and motivate you to pursue your purpose and seek God's plan for your life."

–Abram Doncel
Regional Sales Director, Genentech BioOncology

"Whether you are dealing with a difficult past or are unsure about your future, Never Forsaken will give you hope when things seem hopeless. Juan Ortiz has been a true inspiration in my life for more than two decades. His story of faith, forgiveness and unconditional love will impact your life as well. In addition, this book will be the 'go-to' gift for your friends when you see them experiencing tough times of their own."

–Mike Jakubik
Co-Founder & President , Frontline Insurance Group

"Juan's compelling story is one of perseverance, faith, and resiliency. It highlights the "power of the other" and inspires the reader to think about the unique role he or she can play in another person's life. You will be drawn into the beautiful journey of Never Forsaken."

–Doug McKinley, Psy. D.
Psychologist / Mar̶̶̶̶̶ ̶Xc̶ell̶e̶r̶o̶ ̶L̶e̶a̶d̶e̶r̶s̶h̶i̶p̶ Inc.

"Juan and I are best friends and our families have been doing life together for over 30 years. For that reason, I knew most of the unbelievable stories outlined in this book. It has been amazing to watch as Juan grew through adversity to develop into a successful businessman and motivational speaker. So can you! The principles in this book can change the trajectory of your life."

–Jeff Conrady
Ameriprise Financial, Private Wealth Advisor

"Never Forsaken is a quick read with a lasting impression. Juan's story humbly and powerfully demonstrates that "love is the most powerful force for change in the world."

–Kevin Olsen
Founding Partner, Keyway

"Juan Ortiz appreciates the good in everyone. After reading his story, that is perhaps the most amazing outcome. He has succeeded in business and earned the respect of an entire industry of his peers. But the fact that someone who has endured so much, can approach the world with love and joy, that is truly the happy ending."

–John Rante
Executive Chairman, Blue Pay

Never Forsaken
The Juan Ortiz Story

Never Forsaken

THE JUAN ORTIZ STORY

JUAN ORTIZ AND **JUDSON POLING**

Published by Ortiz Enterprises.
Printed in United States of American
ISBN 978-0-9993658-0-9

Table of Contents

Foreword

IF I INTRODUCED YOU TO JUAN ORTIZ at the local coffee shop you'd walk away thinking you just met a pretty together guy. And for the most part, you'd be right. What you would not see on first blush is that beneath his charming demeanor and delightful sense of humor is a story of courage that has the power to change every life that hears it.

Courage is a word we often use when describing first responders or soldiers who go into battle to protect our freedom. It's the right word. These men and women show up in life's most difficult and dicey moments. They walk into burning buildings and onto battlefields. They attend to those injured at accidents and tragedies. They push back enemies of freedom. They protect the innocent. These men and women know what it feels like to take a deep breath and run toward danger. They choose it and understand what risk is all about. Those of us who benefit from their courage stand on the sidelines of trouble, tragedy or terror and marvel with gratitude at the fiber of their character.

There's another group of individuals I admire as much as soldiers and first responders. The wholeness, healing and freedom they fight for everyday demands a courage many of us don't appreciate. These are men, women and children who learn to take on, and overcome, a threat that is often physically, and always emotionally, hurtful. Their war is waged in what should be safest place on earth…their family. Their battle was not one they choose, it's one that was forced on them. The battle wounds they receive come from verbal and physical abuse…and often, psychological terror that's created by those who should love them most.

Juan Ortiz has fought such a battle, and for the most part, he would tell you he's winning. As a child he struggled to dodge punches thrown by a father who carried past generational wounds and a debilitating addiction. How confusing would it be to hear one day from an inebriated parent, "You are worthless and I'm gonna kill you," and then the next day, in a moment of sobriety, you hear that you are his favorite child? How crazy is that? Imagine what it would feel like to be threatened physically, and intimidated verbally today, and then tomorrow be hugged by that same person. How would that mess with your identity and how you see yourself as you age?

Maybe you know someone like this…maybe you are someone like this. Juan Ortiz is someone like this. How he has managed to face and overcome the insanity of his childhood is stunning and inspirational. Without question, Juan is one of the most courageous people I know and we can each benefit from the contagious power of his courage. Wherever you are currently, Juan's story found in *Never Forsaken*, will break your heart, lift your spirits, make you laugh, and infuse you with hope. It is a story about the power of love lifting a life from tragedy to triumph. It is a story about how God answers prayer and how hope comes from some of the most unexpected places. This story can change the trajectory of every life for the better.

So, let me introduce you to my friend Juan Ortiz through his story of *Never Forsaken*. You will find him brutally honest and as hope-filled as the beginning of a new day. Believe him when he reminds you that your story can be one of overcoming difficulty too. Let him show the way to a place where you can be sure that you are *Never Forsaken* either.

August 2017
Dan Webster, *Founder*
Authentic Leadership, Inc.

Introduction

I PUSHED OPEN THE HEAVY GLASS DOORS to leave the multi-story building where I worked. *Just breathe,* I told myself as I stepped outside. The bright sun and fall colors of this crisp Chicago morning would have been breath-taking—had I any breath left to take away.

For a minute, I couldn't remember where I parked my car. I kept on walking as if some part of me knew. Of course, I did know—it was in the same area I always parked. But the meeting I'd left just moments before rattled me.

I found my car right where my feet remembered it was, and I got in. I took hold of the steering wheel, then noticed my breathing had turned shallow again. I inhaled. *Get a grip,* I thought. I felt a mild, jittery sensation, like too much caffeine.

My arms and chest tightened, so I deliberately relaxed my muscles. I wasn't having a heart attack, but this experience was definitely physical. Was it panic? Joy? Sadness? How could I possibly confuse those feelings? I felt tears welling up. Sitting there in the parking lot, keys in my lap, the previous 24 hours finally caught up with me. I rested my head against the steering wheel. No longer trying to hold it all in, I wept.

How did I get here? I wondered. I had just come from a meeting with my boss, and he had offered me a huge promotion. "Generous" would be putting it mildly; I was set for life. Only the day before, I had proposed to him the terms of my ongoing employment and wondered if I'd be laughed at or reprimanded. I'd consulted with a friend about my plans, worried that my hopes were absurd and selfish. My friend insisted I was worth what I proposed and told me to dream big. I allowed myself to show up with my unedited list of wants because, at the very least, they could be considered an opening offer. My boss was a good man who wanted me to stay, so I knew his counter-proposal would surely be acceptable, even if it wasn't everything I wanted. But he ended up giving me *everything*—everything—I proposed.

There in the parking lot, I cried in elation at my good fortune. Me, ending up here. It seemed an impossible plot twist in my story. Growing up, I didn't have any dreams. I had only nightmares. All I wanted out of life was survive and get away from my family—especially my dad. And here I was: the son of Mexican immigrants, living in a land of opportunity, being hired for a great job with a six-figure income and stock options in a fast-growing company. I was surrounded by talented, high-integrity peers. Most important, I had a loving wife, five beautiful children, a host of great friends and fantastic mentors and role models. How did all this happen to me? How does so much good come to anyone with a past like mine?

For years, people have asked me to write my story. They come up to me after I give a talk in which I share some aspect of my life, and they want to know how they can find out more. Many also say they know someone "who really needs to hear this." It doesn't go to my head because my story is not really about me; it's about all the others who've surrounded, supported and molded me. They form the essential part of my story. I'm sure it would have ended quite differently if they hadn't come along. When I share publicly bits and pieces of the whole story you're about to read (and I can never do any of it justice in a short talk), people are awestruck. Frankly, some of them have a hard time believing it. I sometimes can't believe it either.

The story begins in such a way that you think you know how it's going to end—and it won't be good. When I take stock of where I am now in light of where I started, I can't blame anyone for doubting that it really happened. The truth is, my set of circumstances typically leads to an unfortunate outcome. People raised like me end up like my dad—in prison, or like my mom—married to an abusive spouse, or like so many others with whom I shared my earlier years—succumbing to depression or addictions.

I have an old, wrinkled photograph of my brothers, my dad and me, all grinning while each of us holds one of dad's many illegal guns. At the time we were living as squatters in an unheated, run-down farmhouse. We're brandishing semi-automatic rifles and handguns looking as relaxed and playful as if we posed with Nerf toys. You see the squalor of our surroundings and our mismatched thrift store clothes. You have to imagine the smell—another thing about us that was different (the white kids made sure I knew). There's my dad, a wiry, out-of-control man, who in his line of "work" needed all these weapons—and who figured that a picture of his kids holding them would be a hoot.

Your next thought would be, "Those kids need DCFS to step in!" You'd be right. But we didn't just need help back then; we needed a miracle. And my story is miraculous—though not in a *Touched by an Angel* kind of way. My life demonstrates how simple grace and kindness shown by ordinary people in ordinary circumstances can lead to extraordinary results. It's a story of hope, for other families like mine, or for those who simply *know* people like my family or me, and are trying to help them. It's also a story of hope for our world, because what happened to me is both miraculous and reproducible.

You may be reading this and needing a different kind of hope: a challenge put before you that if you step up to be a guide, like the many caring helpers I had, you really can make a difference. Teachers and mentors truly are the conduit for a better world, and you might be one of them. I'm here to declare that if you get involved with someone like me or my mom—and keep in mind she was married to an abusive, drug-dealer—you can be a signpost to freedom and healing. I hope my story will inspire you to embrace that kind of challenge.

But to tell my story, you first have to meet my mom and dad when they were kids growing up in Mexico.

Chapter 1

Young Love

"HE'S NO GOOD FOR YOU! You must stop seeing him. His family may be rich, but he is nothing but trouble."

The sun was scorching—like it always is in Monterrey, Mexico. Two teenagers—Caesar and his young sister Norma—stood facing each other, trying to stay cool even though it was late afternoon.

"But I love him!" she choked out.

"Love? What do you know of love? You're 14 years old." Caesar was resolved to protect his innocent sister. "You know if mom and dad found out, they would be furious."

Norma stared back at him, on the verge of tears. She pursed her lips, afraid to say more. Young Latina women are taught to respect their family, older brothers as well as parents. This was especially true back in the 1950s. Even though they lived on the outskirts of a modern city, which at the time had over 300,000 inhabitants, this was a traditional Hispanic family. Norma lowered her head. Her family's disapproval seared just as much as the hot dry air. She knew there was nothing she could do to change his mind.

Norma Peña, my mother, was born in 1944 in the state of Neuvo Leon, Mexico. She was barely a teenager when she met Matias Ortiz, two years her senior. Like any young girl, she enjoyed the attention from an older boy. Being from a conventional Mexican family, she hoped to get married someday and have a family of her own. Girls not much older than she was were often already married in that culture. But her family was wary of Matias even before he started to come around to see her. They didn't like him at all. He had a reputation for being arrogant and spoiled. Even worse, at only 14 years old, he sneaked drinks and smoked marijuana.

Norma was one of 14 children born into a dirt-poor but happy family. They all lived in a one-room house. She was a gullible young woman, flattered by the polished charm of an older boy bent on wooing her. A flower of innocent beauty, with green eyes, fair skin, she was admired by all the young men—even in seventh grade. She was also dreadfully naïve. Her older brothers knew that and wanted to protect her.

Matias was the complete opposite. Literally and figuratively, he was from the "other side of the tracks." Born into privilege, he had money, stylish clothes, and jewelry. He certainly appeared to be a catch for any young woman. He went to a private Catholic school and was a straight-A student. His father, Juan, was respected in the community and had worked hard to make his wealth before he got married. (Juan's wife, Manuela, was 15 years younger than he was.) Juan was already 40 when he had his first son, Matias—my dad. But once this apple fell, it rolled far away from the tree. My dad couldn't have been more different than his father.

Matias was cocky and rebellious, a wild child. He began smoking marijuana and drinking at age twelve. When his arrogant streak reared its head, he taunted the nuns at the private school he attended because he was, in some respects, more well-read and more knowledgeable than they were. He could speak several languages. Teachers and others in authority didn't know how to handle him, and he loved to provoke and fluster them.

I have a picture of my dad from at age 10 that serves as a great metaphor of what a contradiction he was. In the photo, he's smiling, smartly dressed in a Boy Scout uniform, poised with a hand on the rail of a staircase, one foot on the step behind him as if he were casually walking down the stairs. It's evident, however, that someone professionally posed him for the picture. His family could afford to pay for such a luxury—another indication of his wealth. He looks adorable, friendly, a son any parent would be proud of. Who would have thought this young man was mouthing off to the nuns at school or would soon be doing drugs?

In another picture from that time—a more typical snapshot no doubt taken by a family member with an inexpensive camera—he is wearing the same uniform, marching in lockstep with a group of other boys, all carrying what look like ceremonial guns. His free hand is pulling back the brim of his hat, as if to say, "You want to take my picture? OK, let me show my face."

Four years after that photo was taken, his brash, conceited ways and stylish, expensive clothes drew the attention of local girls. Lots of girls. Norma's brothers knew of his shenanigans, and they worried that Matias would sweep her off her feet and lead her into his irresponsible lifestyle. It may have been Mexico in the late 1950s, but their romance was a page right out of Romeo and Juliet—the classic young love that flourishes and becomes more resolute under the pressure of family opposition.

Being an older boy, Matias was also "experienced" with girls—despite the deeply entrenched taboo against sex before marriage. He took advantage of Norma before she really understood what was happening to her. When she discovered what that kind of touch meant, it only made her more sure that she was supposed to be with him. Regardless of the morality, the act made her his possession for life, and they were destined to become husband and wife.

In an attempt at privacy, the young couple crouched down behind the yucca plants in front of the one-room house. They knew Norma's parents were inside and had only reluctantly given her permission to step outside to talk to Matias.

"Come with me, Norma," he whispered. "I'll take you away from all this and give you a better life. Marry me, and maybe some day we can move to America where I'll make lots of money." Matias caressed her knees as they sat facing each other.

Even at 16, my dad was a consummate salesman. He could paint any picture he chose, and then get people to buy in. His narcissistic fantasy captivated my mom.

Yet she was torn. Though the promise of making a life with this vibrant young man dazzled her, she loved her family and knew they loved her. Marrying him meant leaving them. Whatever Matias was promising to take her away from wasn't really all that bad. Though poor, she was not unhappy. Having to leave her family to chase a dream with her boyfriend gave her pause. Despite her misgivings, romance intrigued her. She and my dad continued to dream and make plans.

Norma had quit school at 13 and gone to work. Young girls in that culture did not need to pursue an education. Two years later, when Norma was 15 and Matias was 17, their parents realized just how physically involved this romance had become. The only option was to arrange for the two of them to quickly marry. Matias and Norma had a traditional wedding with all the family participating and smiles for the camera. This was the only way to protect their honor in the eyes of the community.

At one point many years later, I asked my mother, "What was it about dad that caused you to fall in love? He had such a bad reputation, and he took advantage of you. Were you mesmerized by his money and bravado, or did you really love him?"

She thought for only a moment before she replied, "I think it was both. Yes, he came from a respected family, and I was flattered by his attention and his social status. But we were both in love—as much as you can be at that age. He treated me good—most of the time, anyway. He had such optimism and energy. So I truly loved him, *and* I was also naive. In my shyness, I just did what people around me thought I should do."

About that time, Matias began boxing as a sport. He had already been involved in athletics, and boxing certainly fit his combative style. For some reason—it may have been related to boxing—he traveled to New York about a year before he and Norma got married. While there, he got into some kind of difficulty with the authorities and was thrown in jail. It wasn't the first time he'd had a brush with the law. Most of the time, his father used his influence or money to bail him out. But for some reason this time, he refused to rescue his son that time. He left him there—for a whole month.

Matias had been a troublemaker before this incident, but when he returned to Mexico, he was a much more violent, angry person. No one knows for certain why he'd been arrested in New York in the first place. Had he been caught with drugs, or aligned himself with a gang? He maintained his innocence whenever he was asked about it, though he never gave specifics. But upon returning, the change in him was noticeable. His sisters speculated that he must have been beaten up or even raped in jail. Some kind of trauma affected him, and he was never the same after. So now, in addition to being arrogant, he'd become violent as well.

Both before and after they got married, Matias was jealous and possessive. His aggravated mean streak only intensified after his New York fiasco, to the point that his jealousy could inflame into rage in mere moments. One time when they were swimming at a local pool, he held Norma's head under the water. She thought he was going to drown her, until he finally let her come up, sputtering and gasping for air. With such ludicrous, cruel displays, he continually asserted his control and wanted Norma to make no mistake about who held the power in her life. She knew enough to recognize such a cruel prank was craziness on his part, but like so often happens when domestic violence occurs, she just tried harder to make him like her—to keep him happy. This destructive pattern started early in their relationship, and it continued throughout their marriage.

When my siblings and I came along, it continued with us.

Chapter 2

The Land of Opportunity

THE HOUSE WAS ALL SHADOWS, except for the glow of a small black-and-white TV. In 1961, San Antonio, television programming stopped at 11 p.m., and the screen switched to a test pattern. The quiet hiss of TV static floated like a wisp of audible smoke in the darkened room.

Outside on the porch, the sound of someone bumping up against the front door broke the near-silence. Keys dropped on the ground. Muffled curses. A moment later, the lock turned, and the door swung open.

A young woman's voice called out from the blackened living room. "Matias? Is that you?" Norma had been asleep on the couch, and she quickly sat up. She rubbed the sleep out of her eyes and squinted to see who stood in the dark hallway.

"Course. Who d'ya think? Werrrre ya expecting one of your boy-friendsss?"

Matias smelled like whiskey. Again. "I have no boyfriend but you! Why do you keep accusing me of that, *mi amor?*"

"I sssee guys look at you. You're exactly the kind of nena they're looking for. Ssstop flirting with them, or I'll make you pay!"

Norma teared up. His crass accusations and threats were completely baseless. But she could never win the argument. Being only 17 and pregnant, she felt even more vulnerable.

She decided to try to change the subject. "I felt the baby move today! Isn't that great?"

Matias didn't even hear her. He was already stumbling off to the bathroom to throw up.

"Please don't wake up *Tia*," she called softly. She turned off the TV and padded off toward the bedroom.

I hope he cleans off the vomit smell this time before he comes to bed.

While San Antonio was pretty much as hot as Monterrey, Mexico, the similarities ended there. America was the land of opportunity, and the young couple moved there shortly after their wedding to pursue Matias' dream. He had just turned 18; she was barely 16. He did odd jobs and learned to weld as well as drive heavy construction equipment. They lived with his aunt, and his young bride stayed at home because she didn't speak English. Without extended family, they never would have made it.

I was my parents' first child, and I came along almost exactly a year after their wedding day. Mom actually gave birth to me in my aunt's house there in San Antonio. Though this was the land of plenty, the doors of opportunity didn't open as wide for a young Mexican couple in America as they did for the white people who surrounded them. My dad was lazy and wanted his father to support him. My parents couldn't make it financially, and they continued to be dependent on his aunt. In his frustration, he started drinking more, smoking marijuana, and staying out late. My mother was left to fend for herself at home. Having a baby gave her something to do and helped her feel some happiness in her otherwise lonely existence.

"Hey Matias! Matias!" A co-worker in a hardhat was trying to get my dad's attention as he sat on his bulldozer. "Matias!" His wave finally got my dad's attention, so he shut off the loud, sputtering engine.

"*Si senior?*"

"Jimmy over there said I should talk to you. I, uh, need a favor."

"OK…" He was hesitant. My dad knew Jimmy, a friend at work, but not this man. And my dad was not in the habit of helping strangers.

"He said you could…" The man stopped and looked around suspiciously. He motioned to my dad. "Lean down! I don't wanna have to shout."

My dad bent toward him.

The man continued in a slightly hushed voice. "Jimmy said you could score me some pot."

My dad wasn't sure if he should say no, and stay out of any trouble, or agree to it. After all, he did have ready sources.

Sensing dad's hesitation, the man added: "Don't worry, I'll pay you well. Can you get it?"

Dad broke into a smile. "*No hay bronca!*" His chest swelled, inflated by the *machismo* from being able to prove himself valuable to this man. Plus, the extra cash could come in handy.

The sale went off without a hitch. Suddenly my dad had a small pile of money—fast and easy. And he realized he could do it again and again. To a struggling teenage parent trying to prove himself in a foreign culture, this seemed like a golden opportunity. In addition to the money coming in, he finally felt like a "somebody"—sought out by others, esteemed even. I'm sure at some level that feeling was a "high" to my dad. He wanted so much to have pride in himself, to command respect. This finally gave it to him. Dealing drugs dominated every major decision Dad would make during my entire childhood.

"Matias! The phone is for you." My aunt called out to my dad, who was sitting on the couch drinking a beer and watching TV.

He took the phone. "*Hola?*"

The voice on the other end of the line spoke. "Matias, you must come home. Papa is very sick." It was my dad's sister. "He is asking to see your son, little Juanito. I think if you all come for a visit, it will help Dad. He may be dying; we just don't know."

I was my grandpa's namesake, his prized first grandson. For some reason, in his sickness, he asked to see me—though I was not even a year old.

"I have to talk to my boss. I don't know if they'll let me go." Dad was conflicted. Despite the drug deals, he still had a day job operating a bulldozer. He was easily replaced, and leaving town might jeopardize his job.

I don't know all the details, but somehow he was able to make it work for the three of us to return to Monterey to visit my grandpa. The amazing thing was that the joy my grandpa felt in my presence actually had a therapeutic effect on him. He got better and was released from the hospital. Both he and my grandma, Manuella, seemed enthralled by me, and they were grateful for how I seemed to affect him so positively.

"Please let him stay. We love little Juanito. You go back to Texas, and we'll take care of him for a while." My aunts who lived with my grandparents were insistent. But my mom did not want to go back to the States without me.

Grandpa also chimed in. "Think of leaving him here as a loan! We borrow him, and then we give him back." Ever the successful businessman, my grandpa was using me to make a deal.

My dad had a different take than my mom. *It's one less mouth to feed. Why not?* "OK, sure," Dad agreed. "You keep him for a couple of months, and then we'll come get him."

Those couple of months turned into almost four years. During that time, my parents had three more children—about one every year I lived with my aunts and grandparents in Monterrey. My parents did come back for visits, but my significant childhood bond was with my grandparents and my dad's two sisters, Katie and Gracie. Grandpa Juan and Grandma Manuella and my two aunts were very religious; they took me to mass every day and prayed for me. The wealth that surrounded my dad when he was growing up they now lavished on me. More importantly for my development, they were unceasingly kind. What few memories I have of those early years are nothing but good. In fact, when my parents came to visit, I was so attached to my aunts and grandparents that I thought of my mom and dad as my aunt and uncle, rather than my parents.

Every time they visited, my mom wanted to take me back, but my aunts wouldn't hear of it. "No! Juanito is staying here with us!" It wasn't that she chose to leave me, so much as they insisted on keeping me. Years later, she confided that she felt utterly powerless when the three of them—Matias and his two sisters—aligned on anything. Yes, I was her child, but with her powerful, well-respected in-law family—who got their way in almost every area of their world—she just didn't have a say, even about her own son. So, reluctantly, she left me there each visit. Truthfully, she knew I was in good hands, so it was some relief to let me go, trusting that I had a better life there than what she and my siblings faced.

My dad was now dealing drugs heavily and living the "on-the-run" lifestyle of a dealer. He made the family move about every six months, in an effort to run from cops or people to whom he owed money. He was constantly getting high or drunk. He carried a gun and wasn't afraid to show and even use it. It's no wonder my siblings' experience of their early years is so drastically different than mine. I had food on the table, toys, stability, and love; my aunts and grandparents—the ones I associated with the parent role—were affectionately involved in my day-to-day life. In contrast, my siblings were raised in a constant state of want, fear, and violence. Psychologists agree the early years of a child are hugely formative for their sense of self and well-being. My earliest years were secure, while my siblings lived in continuous stress and uncertainty.

That all changed, though, when my grandfather died. With him gone, I was "returned" to live with my real parents—though to me, it felt like I was being pawned off on what I considered distant relatives. Right after my grandfather's funeral, I went back to live in the States with my family.

That's when the painful memories begin.

Chapter 3

Life on the Run

"No, MATIAS! PLEASE!" My mom cowered in the corner of the kitchen.

It was late at night, and Dad stumbled around in his drunken fog. He banged into the walls, tipped over the trashcan in the kitchen, and finally grabbed a frying pan. He raised it awkwardly above his head, and it crashed into the cabinet, leaving a dent.

Towering over mom, he snarled, "Where were you at? Huh? What did you do all day while I was out?"

Mom pleaded. "I was here, home with the *niños!* You know I wouldn't go anywhere without telling you."

"Well then who came by? You've been sleeping around. I know it. I bet you did it in our bed, didn't you!"

Mom recoiled. "No one was here. Please, don't… You're going to wake up the kids."

With his free hand, he grasped her hair, and she lurched forward and fell to the ground. He struck her on the back with the pan, and Mom cried out in pain.

Dad stood over her, his rage gaining volume. "I work all day to put food on the table, and you pull up your dress for any man who looks at you twice!" More hits with the pan, more shrieks.

He finally left her in a sobbing pile and looked over at six-year-old me, standing in the doorway. My mom's painful howls had awakened me.

"Go back to bed!" he growled.

"*Papi*, don't hit her!"

"You got a problem, Juanito? You think I don't know what goes on while I'm away?"

"Leave her alone."

"Why do you cover for her? Did she tell you to lie to me?" He turned to mom, still on the floor. "Now you're turning the kids against me! I'll show you what happens to kids who lie to me!"

And just like that, I became his punching bag. Mom cried out, begging him to stop, while the profanity that poured from his mouth in both Spanish and English added verbal barbs to our physical wounds.

Finally, it ended. My mom and I lay bruised and bloody on the kitchen floor. Dad stopped and took stock of what he'd done. I couldn't be sure, but I think he might have had a tinge of regret. As much as I could easily make him out to be some kind of monster, as I look back on it now, I see that he was still human. He showed the full range of truly human feelings—even guilt. Unfortunately, none of those feelings ever stopped him once he was possessed by his rage. So whether he felt bad for what he'd done, or triumphant that he'd put us in our place, when the beating stopped, he headed out of the door to go drink some more.

This was the madness in which my mom and us five kids lived. Day after day, we were chained to a familiar—and nauseating—pattern. Dad would wake up early. Mom made him breakfast. He'd leave for work. Late afternoon, he'd return and demand that my mom cook him something to eat. Then he'd go out again for the rest of the evening. Late at night, after we kids were in bed, he'd stumble home intoxicated. More often than not, he was angry. He'd make allegations about my mom, accusing her of infidelity. But she had her hands full with us kids and wouldn't have had time or opportunity to be promiscuous, even if she'd wanted to cheat on him. My dad's assertions of unfaithfulness were a classic case of projection: he was the one sleeping around all the time.

The pattern more often than not would also include him turning on us kids. As I mentioned earlier, when he saw his whole household cringing and crying, I believe he occasionally felt guilt. He knew he was being such a horrible person. Instead of addressing the problem, he'd go back out and drown his sorrows in more drinking. When he knew he needed to get some sleep before the next day's work, he'd come home. Then his abuse took another turn. He would force himself on my mom sexually (though at the time, we kids didn't understand what that was).

As much as I hated the beatings, I believed if I could tire him out, or at least drain off some of the rage, somehow he wouldn't hurt mom or my siblings as much. Like many abused kids, I tried to step in to "protect" my mom by enduring my father's wrath. I honestly was willing to feel that pain if it might prevent others in my family from experiencing it.

Paradoxically, sometimes when my dad drank, he became affectionate toward me. I can still remember the smell of him up close to me; he made me sit on his lap, he kissed me on the lips, and he told me in sloppy, slurred speech how proud of me he was. He'd then ask, "You proud of me, Juanito? You proud of your old man? *Soy un campeón!* (I'm a winner!)"

What was I supposed to say? No, Dad, I can barely breathe because of the disgusting smell of alcohol on your breath. So I lied. "*Si Papi. Campeón!*"

Like any boy, I desperately wanted his love and approval. But I hated it that he wanted me to call him a winner. That's something a father should say to his son.

Our moving every six months added to the stress and uncertainty. We lived in various places in Texas: San Antonio, Houston, Galveston, Laredo, Mercedes, and Brownsville. We even had a stint in San Francisco, California. There were also trips back to Mexico. Dad was always running from somebody—drug dealers, people to whom he owed money, cops, somebody he'd robbed, husbands of women with whom he'd had sex. He'd come home and announce we needed to move, and in a matter of hours, we'd be packed and out the door. Like snakes sloughing off their skins, we'd leave behind almost all our possessions (along with what few toys we had) in order to make a quick getaway. I barely have any childhood possessions that made it through all those moves, although my mom managed to save the photographs that have helped me piece together our family history.

I have a series of pictures of our family from our time in San Francisco when I was about eight. It's a beautiful sunny day. My mom's hair is made up high into a beehive—typical late 1960s women's hairstyle. In some shots, we are standing by the ocean, and in others we are on a boat. Everybody is smiling, and you would never in a million years guess what was going on behind closed doors. We look like the all-American family, down to the little sailor hats my brothers and I wore. Given that we were always so poor, I'm thinking that my dad must have come into some bigger-than-usual money because we rarely received gifts like that. During our time in San Francisco, I saw my first movie in a theater: *The Jungle Book*. In the photos, we look so happy, so prosperous. It wasn't posed—we were really there, and I know the smiles were real. *Why couldn't life have always been like that?*

We humans are amazingly resilient. We constantly come back to hope: we hope things will get better, we hope people can change, we hope the occasional droplets of love that splash our direction from time to time will someday fill a glass from which we can drink until we're no longer thirsty. My mom kept hoping—despite being beaten consistently. I kept hoping—though nothing about my life was stable. The truth is, most of the time, a relationship with an abuser doesn't work out.

Contrast that hopeful, happy time in San Francisco with what led up to us going there. The reason we had to move was because my dad was running for his life. He'd shot two men in a parking lot in Houston, one of whom was a relative.

It happened just outside a bar, and my dad hadn't seen it coming.

Chapter 4

Cycle of Violence

THE DRUG CUSTOMER SEATED AT THE BAR had a friendly tone, and my dad didn't expect any trouble. Just in case, though, he always carried a .45 revolver, tucked in his pants right in the middle of his back, covered up by his shirt. As they exchanged handshakes, the man my dad was meeting brushed up against both his hips—a poorly masked attempt to check for a gun. (Now you see why my dad kept his gun where it was less likely to be found!) The man's action put my dad on guard.

After they talked for a while, one of my dad's relatives, approached them and said, "Look, let's do this out in the parking lot."

Now my dad was certain: *this is it—they're gonna shoot me.* In the dark behind the bar, there would be no witnesses. They would throw his body in the trunk of their car and drive off, with plans to dump his body somewhere down the road.

Up to this moment in his life, he'd never actually fired his .45 at anyone. For him, it was insurance. Because others knew he carried a gun, it was a deterrent. But in the bar that day, he concluded it was kill or be killed. He told himself, *Well, I knew this day would come. Though I never thought it would be a relative.*

My dad and the other two men left the bar and walked outside to the car. They insisted on my dad going first, which forced him to look ahead and not at them. Just as he reached the car, my dad spun around. Before they knew what happened, he shot them both. They went down. My dad ran to his car and sped off. He didn't know for sure if he had actually killed them, though he later boasted, "I shot 'em enough that they should have died!" He raced home. He grabbed my mom and us kids, and drove at 110 miles an hour toward the Mexican border.

Many years later I asked him, "Dad, why did you drive so fast after that? Speeding would only draw more attention to yourself. I'm surprised you didn't get pulled over."

My dad replied, "If a cop *had* stopped me, it would have been his last day."

As horrendous as his life of drug use and dealing had been, my 23-year-old father now had two attempted murder charges hanging over his head. He later said of that incident, "I was sure then that my life as I knew it was over."

A few hours later, we made it to the border—somehow eluding the police—and crossed into Mexico. Dad went immediately to his supplier.

The man could see my dad was shaken. "Hey, you alright?"

"No, man!" dad yelled. "I just shot _____ and _____!" (naming the two men).

"Oh, OK." The supplier didn't seem upset. But then, why would he? It's just another "day at the office" in that business.

"Give me a minute, I'll be right back." He left the room, and my dad stood there, wondering if now he was in danger from this man. His supplier had known the men my dad shot. Maybe he stepped away to get *his* gun?

The man returned, and handed my dad an envelope. "Here's $10,000."

"Wha—?" My dad's mouth gaped.

"We had a hit on one of those guys. You just took care of our problem."

A pile of money in hand and the family in the car, off we headed to San Francisco. I don't know why dad chose California. Perhaps it was because geographically, it was about as far away as he could get from Houston and still be in the States. But it wasn't long before we resumed the pattern. After about six months, we quickly loaded up a few necessities in the car and headed out to live somewhere else.

Moving so often made me feel like an outsider at school. I was always starting over whenever we got to a new location, but we never lived in a place long enough for me to make friends. Often, no one at the school spoke Spanish, so lessons had to be explained and simplified for me—sometimes, with everyone in the classroom laughing at my "stupidity." It wasn't that I was unintelligent. But how could anyone even know what my IQ was when I couldn't communicate? I rarely understood what was going on. The teachers tried but failed. The kids didn't even bother. With my limited English, mismatched thrift-store clothes, unkempt appearance and unpleasant body odor (our home did not have a shower), I became an easy target. Kids ignored me. A few bullied me. The first day in a new city, I'd get on the bus and, of course, all the kids were strangers. No one sat by me. Though teachers were supposed to be safe, they were also strangers, and they didn't speak my language. I'd often get beat up on the playground before or after school, just because I was "different." On the bus, they'd shoot rubber bands at me and spit on me. Sometimes, my mom would ride on the bus to try to protect me. She got teased as well. What could she do, really? We both just sat there and took it.

In an attempt to protect me from the kids who taunted me, the teachers isolated me in the corner. I'm sure those young, inexperienced teachers didn't know any better—no doubt they thought they were helping. But what message did segregating me send? Based on placement in the room, the only conclusion anyone—including me—could make was that I must be either a dunce or a bad kid. That chair was a picture of how I saw my life: I'm an oddball; I'm an outsider; I'm a nuisance and a nobody. I exist to be teased, marginalized or punished.

After a whole day at school being humiliated, beat up, mocked—or at best, excluded and ignored—I'd head home. Then my dad took over where the bullies on the playground left off. I gradually just became numb to the outside world, to most people (other than my mom and siblings) and to myself. I shut down to survive. The one silver lining of having to move again was relief from the bullies. Every new city and apartment meant I escaped from the torments of my previous school or neighborhood—at least, until the kids in the new location started in on me.

My childhood was bittersweet. The bitter part was Dad beating up my mom, me trying to stop him, then him beating up me as well. The sweet part was after he left the house. In the aftermath of his rage, a strange balm of consolation flowed between us. The violent madness would be over—like the calm after a tornado rips through the neighborhood—and I would crawl over to my mom. Bruised and bleeding, we would help each other up, hobble over to the sink, and wash each other's wounds. I can see my mom's beautiful but pummeled face, as I held her cheeks in my hands and gently dabbed with a warm washcloth each place the skin was broken where she'd been hit by the pan. She'd do the same for me. After the washing, she'd get ice, put it in a towel, and hold it up against my head. As awful as the beatings were, the moments after with my mom made me feel alive, warm, and connected.

Sometimes we remained silent for a while, but eventually Mom would speak up. "It's gonna be OK, Juanito. We're gonna be OK."

"Mom, your forehead is still bleeding."

"Don't worry, it's just a scratch," she'd say, blinking away the drops of blood in her own eyes while she tended to me.

"Juanito, do you know how special you are? You are wonderful. You are handsome." I can still hear her saying the Spanish word for handsome, *hermoso*. No sound was ever sweeter—and it came to me in the most unlikely of settings. In that painful aftermath of being beaten, she told me who I was. She counteracted the messages from Dad and our life circumstances.

She could even find her humor in those moments. "Someday, you're gonna do great things. Remember the three little pigs? The wolf was angry and mean, and he blew their houses down, but the one had a nice brick house. That's you, Juan. You're gonna live in a nice brick house some day. You're my good little piggy! And when you build that house, you'll let us come live with you, right?"

In ways I have a hard time explaining, I felt a strong and deep connection with her while we bandaged each other up. I will never forget those special moments. It was traumatizing to watch Mom get thrown around and beaten by my dad—as awful as being beaten myself. Yet the consolation and kindness she and I gave one another after the beatings helped us keep some semblance of sanity in our otherwise unhinged, unstable life. It showed me that humans can be of immeasurable help to each other in appalling circumstances— even as my dad taught me humans can be the source of unspeakable suffering.

My mother was just an average, young Hispanic woman, caught in a horrific situation. Though confused and conflicted, she did the best she could with meager resources. She was no saint, and yet, in the nightmarish world of my childhood, with all its rejection and pain, she gave me rich pictures of what it means to care for someone else more than yourself. One incident in particular stands out as the most self-sacrificial act I've ever experienced. Though many a mom sincerely believes she would sacrifice her life for her children, on one occasion my mom quite literally lay down on top of me and my siblings and risked her own life to save ours.

It happened on a bitterly cold winter day in Illinois. The whole family was packed in our car, and dad left us sitting outside in a parking lot, ignition off, while he went into a bar to have some drinks.

Chapter 5

Illinois Winter

"Look, there's ice cream everywhere!"

At ten years old, the only weather I'd known was the blistering heat of Texas and Mexico. But looking out the window of our car as we drove the family station wagon toward Chicago, I could see snow everywhere—it blanketed the ground and the trees. From what I could surmise, the countryside in Illinois was slathered with a coating of creamy vanilla goodness.

"There's some on the windows, too!" One of my little brothers started licking at the frost, thinking it was more ice cream. We all joined in, though quickly discovered a wet tongue gets stuck to a frozen window!

Just a day before, we'd been living in Houston. My dad had gone down to Mexico on "business," but the deal went bad. His quick getaway included jumping out of a window onto an awning; incredibly, he escaped with only minor injuries. When he got back to Houston, he told my mom, "I can't do this anymore. I gotta get a real job. I'm gonna talk to my *compañero*, Jerry. He said Ryerson Steel up in Chicago is hiring."

One of my dad's legitimate jobs had been as a welder on the Houston Astrodome in the early 1960s. A buddy of his, who had worked alongside him, was now employed up in Chicago. He'd contacted my dad earlier to tell him about job openings there, but Dad wasn't interested at the time. Terror from the latest drug deal debacle, along with a throbbing sprained ankle, made him reconsider. Things looked different now; it was time for a change. As we'd done so many times before, we got ready for a leave-everything-behind-and-hightail-it-outta-here move. It was mid-February and a balmy 76 degrees in Houston when we threw what we could in the station wagon and set out. We drove straight through, and arrived in West Chicago about 24 hours later.

Where it was *minus* 10 degrees.

Dad drove to the house where his friend lived. I watched him trudge through the snow toward the front door. He knocked. He waited for a while, but no one answered. He walked around the house, looked in a window, and then pounded on it. No response. I could tell my dad was starting to get upset. And cold. None of us had winter coats. We shivered in the summer-weight clothes we'd left with.

As Dad trudged back to the front door, I could see frustration his face. Watching him was a surreal experience for me. On the one hand, I was fascinated with the snowy vista, frosty-framed by the peep-hole my tongue had made on the icy car window. But as an abused child, I always paid attention to where my abuser was and what he was doing. I kept vigilant, even though I was captivated by the delightful winter wonderland. I had developed an early-warning radar system that alerted me when dad's anger was beginning to heat up. One of his distinctive gestures was to grab his hair in frustration—something I catch myself doing now and then. He would also repeatedly slick back his glistening hair with his hands, *el toro* pawing at the ground before a charge.

Finally, a short woman opened the door. Though I couldn't hear anything, I saw her shake her head as if to say, "No, no." Her words upset Dad even more. He stomped back through the snow, got in the car, and slammed the door.

"What's wrong?" my mom asked innocently.

"Nothing!" Dad turned suddenly and punched my mom right in the face. Her nose and upper lip turned red. A few drops of splattered blood froze on the window. She hardly made a sound while she held her nose to stem the flow.

He jerked the car into drive and sped off. He sideswiped a couple parked cars, and swerved back and forth on the road.

"*Estúpido!* Jerry just got arrested for selling drugs! Now we don't have a place to stay. And I don't think he can get me a job while he's in jail."

Dad drove a short distance and then decided to pull over into the parking lot of a bar. He found an open space and nosed in. "You all wait here. I'm going to see if I can get some help for us."

He turned off the engine and got out of the car.

The bitter cold night began wrapping itself around us as soon as dad disappeared inside the bar. When he didn't come out for a while, it became obvious that whatever else he intended to do, he was in there drinking—his standard way to handle overwhelming circumstances. And driving across the country with a wife and four kids only to find out we were all now essentially homeless—as well as jobless in the dead of winter in a strange location—certainly qualified as overwhelming. He wanted so badly to be respected, to be *un campeón*. But this was yet another example of him having to face the fact that he was a failure.

We'd only been out there about fifteen minutes when the bitter cold began to affect us. None of us was accustomed to that feeling, and we didn't know what to do. Dad had the keys, so there was no way to start up the car to provide us with some heat. And even if he hadn't taken them, Mom wouldn't have dreamed of doing anything with the car without getting explicit permission from Dad to do so.

Dad said wait in the car, so we waited in the car. And we started to freeze.

"Mom, what are you doing? I can't breathe!" I gasped.

"We must stay together; that's how we will keep warm." Mom had heard somewhere if you huddle together when you are cold, it helps conserve the heat. So rather than watch her kids shiver any more—and possibly succumb to hypothermia—she instructed the four of us to lie down on the floor of the back seat. I found myself on the bottom of one of two piles when my mom lay across the top of us to keep us warm. I was having a hard time breathing, so we shifted until I could get air. Once we found the right positions, it actually was not all that uncomfortable. Exhausted from the long drive, I drifted off to sleep.

Three hours passed before dad finally came out. At the time, I had no way of knowing just how much danger we were in from the cold. Yet, once we got down on the floor with my mom blanketing us, my siblings and I were protected. Mom, however, was exposed and got frostbite that night. In our family, there was no trip to the emergency room, no doctors, no treatment of any kind. She just had to endure the pain and a slow recovery without the benefit of any medication. Even now when she goes outside, the cold affects her. My heart breaks when I think of how much she suffered, again and again, yet how much she kept sacrificing for us kids. That night, she absorbed the cold and passed on to us her warmth.

Years later I read in the Bible, "Greater love has no one than this: to lay down one's life for one's friends." As a Christian, I believe that's what Jesus did for us. The Bible tells us that when he died he took on the consequences of our sins so we don't have to endure them. Of course, I wasn't there 2000 years ago when Christ did that for me. But I was there on a winter's night in 1971 when Mom literally covered my body with hers to protect me.

When Dad finally got back in the car, he was wasted.

He spoke to us in that familiar, slow slur that too much alcohol gave him. Seeing me in the rear-view mirror, he said, "Hey, Juanito. Come 'ere."

I crawled over the back seat of the car to sit by him.

He put his arm around me. "Hey, you proud of your dad?"

No Dad. I can't stand you. In fact, I hate you. You're an idiot who just put your whole family at risk so you could medicate yourself. We could have died out here. You're a lousy example, a terrible abusive husband, and a self-absorbed narcissist who only cares about himself.

"Yeah, Dad, I'm proud of you." I lowered my head as I spoke.

"I'm a winner!"

He obviously wasn't, or he wouldn't have had to keep telling himself that.

I will give my dad this: he kept trying. He wanted to be a winner and to make us proud of him, and he didn't give up. But he had no leadership, no direction, no one telling him how to succeed. His dad was gone, and he was on his own trying to make a go of it in a foreign culture. And I would have turned out just like him if I hadn't had so many good men who showed me a completely different way to live.

"I'm gonna make you proud of me, you watch."

I cringed, wary of what usually followed the "I'm a winner" routine—intense anger and a beating.

He motioned toward the road. "This guy told me there's an abandoned farm a mile or so from here. We're gonna go there for a few days—three or four, tops—and I'm gonna get a job. We're gonna get a house, we're gonna have nice clothes, we're gonna have cars. You're gonna be proud of your dad, you wait and see." He paused and looked at me. "You believe in me? You trust me?"

"Yeah, Dad, I trust you. I believe in you."

What I believed—what I *could* depend on—was for him to be completely undependable.

We drove down the road a short distance, and there was the driveway that led to a farmhouse set back about a quarter mile from the road. Because of the snow on the unplowed driveway, we couldn't get the car all the way up to the house. We got out and went the rest of the way on foot.

The house was a dilapidated mess. Half of it had collapsed, windows were broken, one of the porch pillars rotted and had fallen down. There was minimal siding, and the inside didn't have drywall—the interior was mostly uncovered insulation. We joined some other homeless squatters living in the house at the time; they seemed okay with sharing the meager accommodations the house offered.

True to form, we didn't stay the three days dad had promised. We lived there for the next three years.

Chapter 6

The Farmhouse

"TONY! LEAVE ME ALONE!"

I was in bed asleep and woke up feeling my brother's hand on my face.

In the run-down farmhouse in West Chicago we were calling home, my three brothers Luis (Louie), Antonio (Tony), and Ricardo (Ricky), and I slept in the same bed. We practically lay on top of each other to all fit. If one of us wet the bed, we all got soaked. When that happened, we could never figure out who the culprit was.

It was bad enough we were crowded together every night, but for some reason in the middle of the night, my little brother Antonio decided to tickle my cheek. My eyes were still closed, and I was groggy.

"I said, stop it! I'll break your fingers."

He persisted.

Angry, I grabbed his hand and squeezed.

Only as I did that, I discovered it wasn't Tony. It was a cockroach crawling across my face.

I bolted out of bed with a yelp and threw the bug across the room. I was fully awake now! Panting, I looked at my brothers. They were still sound asleep. I caught my breath and calmed myself, and I checked the covers for more bugs. Nothing. I crawled back in bed, pulled the covers over my face, and went to sleep.

Life in the farmhouse was unpleasant—just another set of lousy circumstances that I had no control over. I didn't know any different, so I did what I always did: adapted and coped.

At first, we had no working plumbing or central heating. We melted snow on the gas stove for drinking water or to flush a toilet. The stove also kept the kitchen warm enough to live in. Some of the windows were gone; the people who got there before us boarded them up. We covered the open places in the walls as best we could with sheets of thick plastic, though much of the interior was just left open with exposed insulation.

The one bright spot that winter was that we didn't have to go to school. I would have been in fourth grade. No school meant no rubber bands snapped at me on a bus, no getting picked on at the playground. I did kind of miss the coloring I got to do and the picture books. And I missed the teachers who had been nice to me despite the language barrier. But I hated school. I hated the kids and how I was treated. Not having to go was a huge relief.

At some point, the owner of the farm discovered us squatting on his property. He couldn't believe anyone was living in that mess, but he responded with astonishing kindness. He got the water running, replaced some windows and helped to make the place more livable. As it turned to spring and then summer, the warmer weather lured us outdoors. That changed everything. Life on the farm actually became enjoyable for us kids.

Dad brought home a moped one day. I don't know how he afforded it—he probably stole it. But it was a riot. I was the oldest so I drove. Tony sat on the handlebars. Louie was tall and skinny, and we'd tie him to the basket on the back. Gracie, the youngest, sat on the runner. We tried to make it go, but it was too heavy with all of us on it, so it barely moved. Once we did get it moving, with all that weight we couldn't get it to stop. I remember wiping out on the gravel road, falling into a puddle, and Tony rolling into a pricker-bush. We laughed, brushed ourselves off, pulled the prickers out of Tony's skin and got back on.

We were together as a family outside in a beautiful setting. We weren't stuck in a cramped apartment. Nobody teased us. We actually enjoyed life. When the corn came in late summer, we walked through the field and picked the ears and ate them. For all my growing up years, we were almost always hungry. The corn and apples that grew there gave us all a feeling we'd never known before—full stomachs.

Somehow, dad acquired several cars, though none of them were in very good shape. Maybe his customers used them for payment, or maybe he was running a side business buying and selling them. At one point, when one of the cars broke down close to the house, Dad just left it sitting there in our front yard, with the thought that someday he'd have time to tinker with it and get it running again. It stayed there for weeks, so we turned it into a jungle gym. We climbed all over it and then got in it to pretend to drive. Though it had sat there for a long time, low and behold, one morning Dad somehow started the engine. He decided to let us kids drive it, so he got out, and we all piled in.

The 1957 Oldsmobile was the size of a boat. I steered as Tony pushed on the gas pedal, which was a mistake because he liked to go fast. Louie rode shotgun, scared out of his mind, and Gracie braced herself in the back seat. We drove it into the cornfield, up and down the rows, mowing down stalks, shrieking and laughing and swerving. I almost rolled it over by turning too fast. The car finally stalled again right on the edge of the gravel road about 200 yards from the house. This time, it had died for good. We walked back to the house.

"What happened?" Dad asked.

"The car won't go anymore."

"Ay, we were lucky to get it started. It's dead. Just leave it."

A little while later, Dad called us back. "Hey, you know, there's probably still gas in the tank. You guys want to blow it up?"

He wasn't kidding!

He took a sheet and we tore it up into strips tying them end-to-end to make a long fuse. He told us, "Stick it in the gas tank and leave a lot of it hanging out. Make sure all the cloth is wet with gas. Light it. And then run like hell."

We did everything just the way he told us. After lighting it, Tony, Louie and I ran back to the house and waited. But nothing happened. We looked at Dad.

He squinted. "Maybe it went out. Why don't you go back there and light it again?"

As we were walking toward the car, we heard a deafening KA-BOOM! It blew up.

"That was incredible!" We kids shouted and jumped around, doing our best to describe the events of the last two hours.

Dad laughed, a deep laugh that made me wish he could always be like that. The kids raced back to the house.

For us boys, stuff blowing up was fun, not dangerous. But Mom freaked out—understandably. Right after the explosion, she came running out of the house. She started crying when she heard from Dad what had just happened.

"What's wrong Mom?" We couldn't believe our actions had upset her—we thought the whole incident was a riot!

"*Mis hijos!*" She was beside herself with fear and anger, worried we could have been killed.

Dad moved closer to her and puffed out his chest. "Shut up! What's your problem? They're having fun."

Their exchange confused us. Here was Dad, letting us do things other kids were never allowed to do, making life interesting and fun. (He let us do all kinds of risky things, like shoot his tommy-gun at the barn, even though I fell over backward from the recoil, still holding the trigger as it fired into the air.) In a twisted way, he was doing what dads are supposed to do: mentor us kids in the ways of adult life (though his version of adulthood was dangerous and destructive). But Mom was terrified of how he constantly put us in harm's way. So when he was being the most fun and "nice" to us, she was the angriest with him out of her fear for us. What does a kid do with that?

I don't know the exact arrangements my dad had with the farmer who owned the property, but the man eventually started charging us to live there. That angered my dad. "How can you charge us rent? This place is a dump!"

"I never intended for anyone to live here. But now that you are here, I think it's only fair."

"We pay for the utilities. What's it costing you for us to be here? *Nada!*"

"I got the water running for you and put in windows. And it's a roof over your head."

"Big deal. That's maintenance you should have done anyway to keep things from getting worse."

"Look, if you don't like my terms, find someplace else to live."

"We're helping you. What if something unfortunate happened? We can protect your property from vandals." (Wink, wink.)

"Look, I don't want any trouble. What I'm asking is reasonable. Pay up, or move out."

What got my dad especially frosted was that the farmer considered the barn on the property as part of what we were renting—it was a package deal. True, the barn was in great shape, and the farmer himself used it for storage. We played in it, too. But we really had no use for it, so my dad tried to get him to lower the rent so we were only paying for the house. But the farmer's logic was, it was a farm, and the farm included the barn.

The farmer wouldn't budge. Bad idea when dealing with my dad.

When the farmer left, my dad went back in the house. We kids were playing in the yard.

As the sun got low in the sky, Dad came back out. He was clearly still angry, and now we could see he was also drunk. He swaggered over to the barn and went in. We just kept playing, hoping he'd leave us alone.

A few minutes passed and Dad came out. He had a smug look on his face. He stopped, turned around, and stared at the barn. We kept playing, even though our radar was on high alert, as it always was when he was anywhere near us. What was he up to?

Smoke started coming out of the door, a little at first, but it quickly began to billow. Dad smiled with sick satisfaction.

"You want to charge me rent for a barn? I'll show you, *pinche gringo?* There is no barn anymore!"

We stared at the growing inferno, mouths hanging open.

My mom came running out, screaming at my dad. If she'd gotten close enough to him, he'd probably have swatted her like he always did when she mouthed off. But she kept on running past him, past us, all the way down the quarter-mile or so to the main road. She headed right into the middle of the busy highway and tried to flag down someone to call the firemen. *"Fuego! Ayúdenos por favor!"* ("Fire! Help us please!")

This tiny Mexican woman waving and yelling in the middle of the highway while cars and trucks whizzed by was quite a sight. Somebody eventually stopped. Mom didn't let the fact that she couldn't speak English stop her. She frantically pointed back toward the barn, now engulfed in flames. When the guy saw what was happening, he jumped back in his car and sped off to notify the emergency services.

By the time the firemen got there, a small fire had spread to the roof of the house, which they quickly put out. The damage to the house was minor. The barn was a total loss.

Everybody left, and then my mom lit into my dad. I'd never seen her so angry. *"Tu eres un idioto!"* She was mostly upset that he endangered us kids. Without thinking, she started pounding her fists on him.

Dad would have none of that. He dragged her back into the house and beat her up.

No one could prove my dad had set the fire. Mom and us kids couldn't speak English so we were never questioned. Dad wasn't telling anybody anything. I'm sure the landlord must have had his suspicions. Maybe the insurance money was enough to satisfy him. I have no idea if Dad ever paid any rent, but I do know it continued to be our home even after that incident.

Chapter 7

Guns

"MAMA! COME QUICK! JUANITO'S HURT!"

My little brother Louie burst into the farmhouse door. My mom quickly threw down her dishtowel and ran after him. Dad had parked several cars—now abandoned—on our property, and we'd been playing on them. We had been jumping from car to car and sliding down the windshields. On one windshield, the wiper blades were pointed up instead of parallel—and the stub had no rubber blade. When I slid down, my leg met the jagged, rusty metal, which went into my flesh like a shish kebob. The wiper was attached to the car so it wouldn't break off as I wiggled trying to get free. I couldn't get enough leverage to climb back up the slick glass to pull my leg off of it. I was skewered, howling in pain and bleeding, unable to get down off the car.

Oye! Juanito! Qué te has hecho? ("What have you done to yourself?) I imagine Mom must have been terrified, but as most mothers know, when your child is hurt or in danger, you can do whatever it takes to save them. Mom climbed up on the roof of the car and somehow pulled me up off the wiper-blade holder. Then she helped me hobble back to the house.

As always when one of us got hurt, there was no hospital. No doctor. No medicine. My dad helped my mom wash the wound. They taped the gash closed as best they could. The pain permeated my body, but I just had to endure it. I still see the scar to this day, and though it's only an inch or so now, it was much bigger as a boy. I sometimes weep when I think back to all the pain I had to endure because I had no other option.

Physical wounds were just a part of our lives—accidentally caused or from beatings. My dad hit me in the face one time, and the resulting wound got infected. My jaw just blew up—it looked like there was a giant cyst. I couldn't even open my mouth. My dad took a needle, heated it up on the stove, and lanced it. Even with it cleaned out, I was in agony. We never went to the doctor or got any medicine. I can remember crying in bed at night from the pain.

Here's the weird part. The most physically painful experiences I remember from my childhood were not the beatings—not the cuts and bruises. No, the greatest pain was *being hungry*. To this day, that's what grieves my mom the most when she talks about life back then. Typical childhood injuries are one thing. But to see your kids crying because they are hungry, to hear them plead "Mom, my stomach hurts so bad!" when there is literally nothing in the house to give them; that's her living nightmare. I have children of my own, and I cannot imagine the torture of seeing them in that kind of need and be powerless to do anything to alleviate their suffering.

Our world was filled with contradictions. Though my dad would beat up mom when he was drunk, when he was sober, he could be a romantic husband. It was not uncommon for Dad to take my mom dancing in the evenings. When they left the house, they put me in charge of my siblings. They always stayed out late and never got home before we were asleep. That part was okay. But on a few occasions, they didn't come home at all. I was left alone for a day or two to feed and take care of my siblings. On those nights when I was in charge, I turned on the TV until everyone was asleep on the couch. Then I'd wake them up and make them go upstairs to bed. I usually wanted everybody to sleep in my parents' bed because it overlooked the entrance to the property where I could see if anybody was coming. Every now and then, because the house looked abandoned and was in the middle of nowhere, teenagers would drive onto the property and yell and do crazy stuff. That's when being just a kid home alone in charge of four younger siblings terrified me most. I also imagined bad guys—or the police—would come to find my dad. I knew enough about his dealings and violent streak to realize that he had enemies. I'm sure there were many who wanted him dead. I always locked the doors and turned off all the lights. I'd stay awake as long as I could, looking out the window. One time a car came right up to the house. I couldn't see clearly enough to make out faces. But bodies were moving around, and someone knocked at the door. They jiggled the handle, then walked around to the back of the house and knocked there, then peered in the window. Petrified, I held still, barely daring to breath. Angry, gruff voices muttered something. They got back in the car and drove off.

Mom hated leaving us alone at those times. Dad didn't seem to care. He would frequently take mom and drive the hour or so into Chicago to party in the Latino and black neighborhoods of his friends. I'm sure some of these trips were also "business-related" because almost certainly the people Dad hung out with were customers or suppliers for his drug dealings. After drinking, smoking and gambling, it would be too late—or he was too wasted—to drive all the way back out to the suburbs to the farmhouse. They came home the next day. Or whenever Dad felt like it.

At times, my siblings and I could appear to be normal kids doing normal things kids did in 1960s America. I do have fun memories, like when my brother Louie collected Bazooka bubble gum wrappers to get a camera.

FREE! REAL CAMERA. Takes 16 photos to each roll. #127 film prints can be enlarged with instructions. Year round fun. Send 250 Bazooka comics or 50¢ & 10 comics.

We saved all the ones we got and dug through trash everywhere trying to find more. Eventually we saved enough to mail them in. Just as promised, they sent a camera in the mail. It was a cheap plastic toy—it barely worked—but today I have pictures of that farm because of that camera. They are the fixed memories of my childhood, and among the few family pictures that survived our crazy life.

The property was home to a couple of ponds and a lake. None of us knew how to swim, but we weren't afraid of the water, so we waded in and splashed around. We probably should have been more concerned that we might drown, but we made some great memories.

One summer's day, the five of us kids walked into the house soaking wet. Dad was in a good mood for some unknown reason.

"You kids having fun out there?"

"Yeah. But we want a boat for the pond!"

"A boat! Hmm. You know what? That oil tank on the side of the house is empty. I bet it would float."

"Really? That would be cool!"

"Let me help you get it off the wall."

Dad got his tools, and in no time, he cut it loose. We taped up whatever holes we could find with duct tape, and then started rolling this huge oil tank out to the pond near the front entrance to the property. It took forever for us to get it there. But when we pushed it into the pond, it did indeed float! We fearlessly jumped on it and, somehow, didn't hurt ourselves or fall off it in the deeper water and drown. I do remember one time Tony jumped in and couldn't get his foot out of the mud. He waved his hands, but his face was under the water. I saw he was in trouble and jumped in to pull him out. We were much more careful about the muddy bottom of the pond after that!

Our "play" was often more dangerous than we realized. We used to sit up on the roof of the chicken coop and watch the planes pass overhead as they took off or landed at the nearby municipal airport. One time, there was an airshow at the airport, and it was really busy with planes continuously taking off, landing, and doing stunts. Because of how the runway was situated, planes flew over our property as they prepared for another run over the airport where a huge crowd was watching. My brothers and I took some of my dad's guns up there that day and tried shooting at the planes! I know now that the 12-gage shotgun wouldn't have done any damage to a plane flying even low overhead—the range just wasn't enough. But we also had a military M1 that my brother Louie shot at a twin-engine plan that came very close to us! A bullet from that gun could have severely damaged a plane, or worse, wounded or killed the pilot. And if the plane then crashed into the crowd of people, we could have

Guns
43

caused a disaster. I'm sure it is by the grace of God that we didn't
harm anyone that day.

Dad continued to support the family in his crazy way. He occasionally got jobs welding, but he dealt drugs to make his real money.
He liked to have people over, which seemed odd given the run-down
condition of the farmhouse. I would think he would have been
embarrassed to let people see how we lived. Those "parties" were
probably just extended drug deals, and I suppose the people he had
over didn't think much of it because they didn't live in fancy houses
either. When people came for dinner, everyone would get drunk.
Eventually, people would begin to yell, then push and shove. A fight
would break out. Watching men shout at and punch each other at
close range is terrifying, especially for a little kid.

One time my mom made a nice dinner for another couple. The
man and my dad started drinking, and before long it got ugly. My
mom saw the escalation and had me grab my siblings and shuffle
us all upstairs. I made sure they stayed put, but I was curious. I
walked back down to the bottom of the stairs and hid behind a corner where I could see what was going on. From my vantage point, I
could only see my dad, but when I peeked out around the corner, I
could see the other man too. Dad said something that angered the
man, and he responded by standing up and pulling out a knife. Bad
idea. My dad reached behind him and grabbed his gun out of his
waistband. He shot the other man twice—once in the stomach and
once in the shoulder. He was aiming for the guy's head and heart,
but he was so drunk he missed.

The sound of a .357 magnum going off in a house, at close range,
is a terrifying sound—probably the scariest thing I ever heard
during my childhood. The man's wife was screaming. My mom was
screaming. The guy had fallen to the floor where he moaning in pain,
but he wasn't dead. Terrified, I ran upstairs,

My siblings were all screaming. "What happened? Is mom okay?"

I tried to calm them down. "It's—it's okay, okay! Everybody's
okay."

My dad came to his senses and realized he'd over-reacted. He
picked the guy up, put him in the car and drove him to the hospital.

The man made a full recovery—though why my dad didn't get into trouble with the authorities, I can only speculate. I've often wondered if he had connections somewhere, because he seemed to be able to get away with things I now realize should have resulted in the authorities putting him behind bars.

Seeing Dad shoot another man deeply affected me. It made it all the more terrifying the one time he pulled a gun on me. He'd been yelling at me for something—I don't even remember what—and I wouldn't cry. Screams, hits, threats from him, but no tears from me. He exploded with rage when he saw I wasn't breaking down.

"Why won't you cry? You think you're a tough guy, huh? You think you can stand up to your old man?" He pulled out his gun and held it right up to the side of my head.

I lost it. "No, Dad, no! Please! Don't shoot!" I wasn't merely crying now; I was sobbing—deep, guttural sobs.

My mom came into the room and shrieked in terror.

Dad was undeterred. "Yeah, now look who's tough! Who's the cry-baby now?"

It seemed like forever, but it was probably only a few seconds. Dad pulled the trigger.

Click.

The gun wasn't loaded.

I sat there on the couch in shock. Mom stood just behind Dad, wailing in combined rage and fear. My tears stopped, but I panted in shallow gasps like a dog. Immobilized, I shook like a leaf in the wind, my eyes staring out into space.

Immediately, Dad started crying. "I'm sorry, I didn't mean to do that! I love you, Son!" He put his arms around me, but I still couldn't move for the longest time.

Another time my dad came home drunk one afternoon. His words slurred as he tried to warn us. "Look…there's gonna be a problem here. Someone is gonna come to the house. Don't say nothin'. Just keep your mouths shut!" Then, he went upstairs and cut a hole in the drywall ceiling. He collected all his guns and put them up in that opening. Once they were tucked away, he replaced the drywall piece, patched it up and painted it. The rest of the walls and ceilings throughout the house were such a hodge-podge of different surfaces, makeshift coverings and partially-finished drywall, that his handiwork didn't stand out at all. Then Dad left.

Later that night after supper, I heard a commotion outside. I looked out the window and saw a bunch of squad cars with flashing lights and several other unmarked police cars racing down the half-mile gravel road that led from the main highway up to the farmhouse. They pulled up to the house. Doors swung open, and out of all those cars swarmed a hoard of police officers all over the front lawn, guns drawn. One had a bullhorn.

"Matias Ortiz! Come out with your hands up. You're surrounded!"

I thought Dad was still gone, but he'd come home sometime after supper. He suddenly appeared in the living room and calmly walked out through the front door to meet them.

As soon as he reached the porch, the police moved in. They pushed him down and handcuffed him.

"What have you got on me? You don't have nothin'!"

Somebody had apparently turned in my dad for his possession of so many guns, most of which were illegal. It could have been a neighbor, or someone who wanted to get my dad in trouble. Heck, maybe a pilot had reported somebody shooting at his plane from the ground below!

While some of the officers were with Dad on the porch, other men came in and gathered our whole family to ask us questions. Mom simply cried while she held little Ricky on her lap. We sat wide-eye, terrified, like trained dogs sitting obediently in a row on the couch. They didn't have an interpreter with them, so it became clear pretty quickly that their English wasn't getting through to mom—though I actually understood English pretty well by now and knew what they were asking. Dad kept shouting at us from the porch, "Don't say anything! You don't have to talk to them! If you open your mouths—"

Mid-sentence, an officer kicked him, and he fell silent. After a few seconds, he continued. "If you say anything, I will kill each one of you!" Another blow and some threatening words. But Dad had made his point. We stayed completely silent.

The officers started combing through the house, going into every room, looking behind what little furniture we had, moving everything that wasn't bolted down. We could hear they were still roughing up Dad outside. It surprised me that I actually felt bad for my father and angry with the officers. I wanted them to stop hurting him.

One of the officers found a suspicious box, and brought it out to Dad and the other police who were with him.

When Dad saw it, he yelled, "Don't open that! Get it away from the house; there are kids in there!"

Now they thought it was a bomb or some dangerous chemical and really started laying into my dad, punching and threatening him. "Why don't you want us to open that? What's in there?"

But Dad wouldn't tell them.

A special detail of men took the box out on the front lawn. Carefully, they opened it up. It was nothing more than a plastic box with an old record player in it! Beat up as he was, Dad had fooled them. They pummeled him even more.

They stayed a while longer, but no one found anything to get my dad in trouble. When they realized they weren't going to get any incriminating evidence, they all packed into their cars and hauled Dad away. Dad's trick of hiding the guns in the ceiling worked.

Dad returned home the next day. He was right; they had nothing on him. He was off the hook.

Just another day in the Ortiz household.

Chapter 8

Mr. Lowery

"HELLO. I NAME JUAN ORTIZ. My mom…she would like to go to school."

I stood at the counter in the office of Turner Elementary Grade School holding my mom's hand, with my four siblings behind us. I was so short that my eyes barely peeked above it. In my uncertain English, I was trying to tell the principal that my mom had brought us kids to register for school. I was pretty good at understanding English by now, but I didn't really speak it. I often miscommunicated when I tried.

We had been at the farmhouse for about six months. We had not attended school since leaving Texas. Maybe because she'd seen all the school buses on the road, but somehow Mom knew it was time for us kids to go back to school. I entered fifth grade having skipped the last half of fourth grade (unless you count being "home-schooled" by my dad in subjects like, "Off-Roading for Pre-teens" and "Makeshift Floatation Construction" and "Intro to Military-Grade Firearms"). I don't know how Mom knew where the school was. But on a bright day in September, she got all five of us kids dressed and ready and we walked out the front door and down the driveway.

When we reached the busy street at the end of our half-mile driveway, Mom turned left and motioned for us to follow. This was the "country," and there were no sidewalks. Cars whizzed by at 55 miles an hour while we walked on the gravel shoulder. After about a mile and a half, we turned to go south. I don't know how she knew where we were, but we walked down that road for about another mile. Thankfully, we had reached a residential area, so the situation wasn't as dangerous now. We kept walking.

Eventually, we arrived at Turner Elementary School and entered through the large, glass front doors. A woman in the hallway saw us and gasped. Her shocked expression told the whole story. We looked pathetic. We wore dirty, mismatched clothes—the same ones we'd worn since leaving Houston in February—and had lice in our hair. On top of that, we were coated with road-grit recently added by our three-mile trek to get there. My mom tried to tell the woman—in Spanish—that she wanted to enroll us kids in school. The woman gave a polite smile and said she didn't speak Spanish. She turned and started to walk away.

My mom started crying. *"Necesitamos ayuda, por favor!"* (We need help, please!) She continued in Spanish, now crying out to no one in particular, "I hate our life! I hate your father for bringing us here. We need help, and nobody understands us!"

It really got to me to see her so upset. I took a risk and spoke up. "Hello! I name Juan. We need help."

"Oh, so you do speak English! What a relief. I was just going to the office to see if anyone knew Spanish. Don't worry; everything will be fine. Bring your mom and brothers and sister and come with me." With some simple hand gestures, she got us to follow with her into the main office.

"Did you mean your mom brought you here to go to school, young man?" The polite smile told me the administrator behind the counter was either genuinely concerned, or she thought my Spanglish was amusing.

"Yes. My mom wants *us* to go to school."

"OK. Well, welcome to Turner Elementary! How old are you?"

"I am Juan Ortiz. I am 10."

"And the others?"

"Others?"

Motioning to my siblings, "Your brothers and sister, right?"

"Oh, my brothers and sister. Yes. This Louie. He is eight. This Tony, he is seven. Gracie, six. Ricky, one. And my mom, Mrs. Ortiz. She is…(I had to think), um, *old.*"

"OK. Glad to meet you Mrs. Ortiz." She reached out her hand to shake it, but Mom had little Ricky strapped to her chest and had a hard time reaching back to her.

"Well, Ricky is too young to go to school. But all of the rest of you, come with me."

She led us all to a back room. She gave me a clipboard with paperwork. "Here you go, Juan. Can you fill this out?"

"I don't…uh, only a little bit English."

"I know, Dearie. Just do the best you can."

The form might as well have been written in Japanese. We had so many hurdles to overcome—and that form felt like another barrier. We needed help—not papers shoved in our face. I know she didn't mean to be cruel, but it's meaningless to "do the best you can" in such circumstances. I don't speak English. I don't write English. I can't even sign my name. And it wasn't that any of us lacked intelligence. Not speaking the language is not the same thing as being stupid.

Unfortunately, I see so many people—educated people, even people who profess religious faith—who treat people from a different culture with a complete lack of sensitivity. There is a way to offer assistance to people like us with dignity—where it's understood that patience and grace are needed, but also that you're dealing with capable people who just aren't familiar with all the terms and procedures that are second-nature to you. Someone showed you how things work and now you have the opportunity to do that for them. Foreigners in need haven't had the guidance you take for granted. Next time you see someone like my family, remind yourself that you'd be the same way if you lived in the same circumstances. And with a little help, they can go just as far as you—maybe further. They aren't asking for *more* than you got or even special privileges. They just want a fair go.

Once we settled in the nurse's office, they had the four of us kids take off our clothes. Mom was freaking out and didn't understand what they were doing. They tried to reassure her nothing bad would happen. It was very humiliating. They had us stripped down to our underwear in front of each other and these strangers. They put on gloves and began to clean us off with damp rags. They shook out our clothes as best they could, hoping to get rid of not just dirt but lice.

We got dressed again, and they took my siblings and me to class-rooms, one by one. When they got to me, the woman—I think she was the principal—led me down the hall to a big wooden door with a small window cut into it. She knocked at the door, and I could see the teacher walking over. When she opened it and saw me, she had the same shocked reaction. A gasp, eyes like saucers, hand up to her mouth, trying to stifle herself. By now, I was getting used to people responding this way.

I know. We're different. There's something wrong with us. Not really sure what it is. Sorry to have to put you through this, I thought to myself.

"Hi, this is a little boy named Juan. His whole family just showed up, and we're not sure what to do. They don't speak English. Could you do me a favor and keep him here in your room?"

The teacher agreed and did what every other teacher did. She put me in a desk by myself off in the corner. The "different kid" zone, where sight lines are unobscured and the whole class can stare at the dirty Mexican who can't talk. A few of the kids snickered.

"Let's everyone be nice to Juan."

One of the more outspoken kids near me couldn't contain himself. "He *smells!*"

"Now, we'll have none of that!" Her protest was pretty fee-ble—I'm guessing she'd thought the same thing but knew enough not to say it out loud. She put a few papers in front of me, along with a pencil. As she turned and walked to the front of the classroom, a kid snapped a rubber band at me. Truth be told, it didn't affect me. No anger. No tears. No facial expression. *Whatever. You're not the first class to tease me.*

But after a while, I found myself wondering: *What is life about? Really, why am I here? Why do I have to deal with this and these other kids don't? My dad is a loser. I'm sure he's gonna kill us—it's only a matter of time. Is there a point to any of this?*

When the school day was over, I discovered my mom waiting in the hallway for us. She had stayed there the whole day. After she gathered the four of us from each of our classrooms, they put us on a bus and drove us home. And now that they knew where we lived, the bus was there every morning to take us to school.

The next year, sixth grade, I had a wonderful teacher named Mr. Lowery. He knew we were a problem family, and that I was a troubled boy. He was a fantastic teacher, who at one time had considered becoming a priest. Every day he would tell me the same thing. "You are special. You are smart. You are a wonderful young man." His concern was genuine. With attention and kind words, he attempted to rebuild my pummeled self-esteem.

Kids wouldn't play with me at recess, but sometimes Mr. Lowery would come out and kick the ball with me. He got some kids to play with me, too (though when he wasn't around, they didn't do it on their own). When he saw that I sat by myself at lunch, he tried to get some of the kids to join me. Noticing how rarely I changed my clothes (obvious by both sight and smell), he brought me some new shirts and pants. In a generous turn on the typical practice of giving the teacher an apple, Mr. Lowery brought *me* fruit from time to time. He even found a used bike and brought it to me at the farm.

I'm sure other teachers tried to help me, but I don't remember those moments—only their failures. Some kids were probably nice to me, but I would have judged them as fake, and so I don't remember them either. But Mr. Lowery persisted. He kept after me, and seemed to have limitless patience and generosity. So I do remember him and that amazing year he was my teacher.

I also remember not knowing what to do with that no-strings-attached concern. No man had ever shown me any kindness (other than my grandpa so many years ago back in Mexico). It didn't make any sense to me, and I kept wondering why he would be so good to the grimy little Mexican kid. Yet inside, I loved it. It reminded of what my mom told me. For reasons I don't fully understand, I found it difficult to show my appreciation. I never thanked him or outwardly let on that he was making me feel something warm inside. I just couldn't find it in myself to trust him. So I did what so many abused kids do: I shrugged it off because there wasn't enough room inside my shriveled soul to hold what he gave. My heart had contracted, and hardened. It was going to take a lot to make it soft again—to allow it to expand so love like that could have a place inside me to make a home.

When I left sixth grade, I never went back to see Mr. Lowery. I never thanked him. I never let him know what a fantastic male role model he was. He gave me one of the greatest gifts of my childhood, but he never knew what he meant to me.

Thanks to the kindness and persistence of Mr. Lowrey—and some other delightful people you're about to meet—the trajectory of my life slowly began to head in a new direction.

Juan's father, Matias, as a young boy at home. He grew up in a well-to-do family, but had a reputation as a trouble maker.

Matias marches in a parade in Mexico as a youngster

Matias, age 17, and Norma, age 16, were married in Monterrey, Mexico on November 26, 1960. They moved to the United States shortly thereafter.

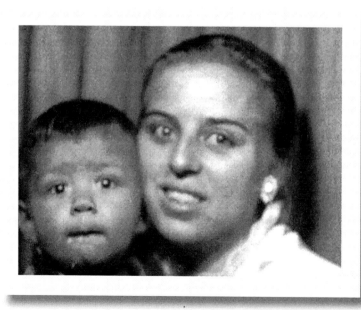

One-year-old Juan and his mother Norma pose for a photo during a visit to Mexico, where Juan was living with his grandparents—an arrangement Norma simply had to accept.

"Really? I have to sit on a plastic donkey? Isn't there another way to celebrate my birthday?" Juan looks very skeptical on his first birthday in Mexico.

Louie, Tony, and Juan stand in front of his grandparents' home in Mexico during a visit. Juan lived with his grandparents, while his siblings lived with his parents.

Norma and Matias go out dancing while living in Texas. The young couple, ages 23 and 24 in this photo, already had four children by this point.

One of the stray dogs stands on the porch of the abandoned farmhouse in West Chicago where the family lived. Norma would take scraps from the garbage at her job as a dishwasher, and bring them home to feed both the ten stray dogs that hung around the property, and her six children.

Inside the abandoned farmhouse where they lived, Norma and the children gather for a family photo. Tony (in the hat), Juan, and Gracie are on the right. Louie holds baby Ricky.

The Ortiz children: Tony and Grace (back row), Juan, Ricky, and Louie (left to right, front row).

Matias posed his family with six of his many illegal (and likely stolen) weapons. Gracie and Tony stood on a bed holding shotguns, while Norma held a shotgun in one hand and baby Ricky (brandishing a German Lueger) in the other. Juan (center, front) held a machine gun while Louie held a military M-1 rifle.

Ricky, left, Gracie, and Juan pose on the roof of one of the many abandoned cars that the children used as a playground, hopping from car to car (and often getting seriously injured). Louie took the photo with a camera he got by mailing in bubble gum wrappers.

TURNER SCHOOL

MR. KENNETH FRY, PRINCIPAL
MR. LOWERY - GRADE 6

1973   1974

Mr. Lowery, Juan's sixth grade teacher, was a light in the darkness of his life. His kindness was never forgotten.

Becky and Juan during their senior year at Trinity University, 1984. She was a cheerleader; he played soccer. They married after graduation.

The Ortiz children and their mother, all grown up. Louie (front left), Tony, Juan (standing), Gabriel and mom Norma (second row), Gracie, and Ricky.

Juan and Becky and their children pose for a family Christmas portrait, 2016. Front row, left to right: Lauren, Michelle, Heather. Second row, left to right, Steven, Becky, Juan, Philip.

Chapter 9

When Grace Came Knocking

IN FALL OF SIXTH GRADE, I came across an announcement that there would be football tryouts for the West Chicago Park District "Chiefs." I didn't realize what a big kid I had become, though I do remember that about that same time I started fighting back when kids picked on me. Getting beaten up at home toughened me up, so boys my age hitting me was not that intimidating. Though I was never one to start a fight, if anyone pushed or shoved me, I took them on. Even my younger siblings felt safer with me around, and used me as their hammer: "If you hurt us, my brother Juan will beat you up!" And because the teachers typically arrived after the fight had begun—when I was on top of the kid who'd picked the fight—I started to get a reputation as a problem kid with "anger issues." To this day when I watch a football game and see one player start a fight, and the other player who was simply defending himself get penalized, the injustice makes me get out of my chair and yell at the referees.

When the announcement for tryouts came, Todd—one of my few friends—said, "We should see if we can play football."

I didn't know what football was—I'd never seen it. But when Todd talked about how you get to smash into other players and tackle them, I thought it might be fun. So I tried out for football, not knowing if I would make it.

I told my mom about what I was doing. She didn't understand what football was either, but she hesitatingly gave her approval. Dad did not. "You can't play!" he said. It wasn't about the game—it was about the cost of uniforms and shoes, which he knew we couldn't afford.

Despite Dad's objections, I tried out anyway. Todd and I both made the team. Now I had the problem of getting equipment. When Todd's family found out about my situation, they kindly paid for everything I needed. I told Dad that it wasn't going to cost him anything, so he changed his mind. I started to play football and really enjoyed it.

Except for dealing with Dad, my only ride to games. Because he was drunk most of the time, he usually forgot when I had a game. After I suited up in my gear, I ended up waiting and waiting for him to come home and drive me to the field. When he finally *did* get home, he never said he was sorry. He'd bark at me to get into the car and then drive me to the game. We would often get there when the game had already started. It was so embarrassing—and to this day, I *hate* being late to anything.

I wasn't a good player, but our team did well. We got to travel to Ohio to play a game there. The team stayed with families who were willing to put us up. I got to see, from the inside, how a few other people lived. The family I stayed with had so many nice things, and they all seemed to treat each other with kindness and respect. I already felt different. This just underscored that I was an outsider looking in at the rest of the world. I was also self-conscious of what they thought when they saw me and realized who they had to host a big, smelly Mexican kid who struggled to speak English, wore clothes that didn't match, and seemed socially awkward, to put it mildly.

Nevertheless, football opened up a whole new world for me. Here was a playing field—literally and figuratively—on which I could compete and be an equal. Suited up, my clothes looked like all the other boys'. Once the game started, they all got just as dirty as I did. The guys I was playing with actually wanted me to be there. When I made a good play, my teammates and coaches gave me slaps on the back—so different from the "contact" I was used to at home.

Dad continued in his erratic, twisted behavior. One night after we'd all gone to bed, he was drunk and started fighting with my mom. I woke up, and lay there wondering what I should do. I got out of bed and came downstairs to help. Even though Mom was holding a baby, Dad violently pushed her down on the living room couch. I couldn't stop myself and got in the fray. Then the other kids came down too—the whole family was there.

My mom finally said to my dad, "Why don't you just leave us alone! Stop all this—go away and let us live in peace!"

Dad paused for a second, seeming reflective. He then walked across the room, grabbed a chair and turned back toward us.

"Alright, everybody sit down. I figured out our problem."

We all sat on the couch, and he brought the chair over and plunked himself down on it facing us.

"You know what our problem is?"

I wanted to say, *You are the problem!* But I didn't have the nerve.

He continued: "Actually I figured out *your* problem. And you know what it is?" He paused for dramatic effect. "Your problem is *me.*"

Mom said, "What are you talking about?"

"Nah, I realize the problem is me. If you guys didn't have me, you wouldn't be in this mess. But tonight…tonight, we're gonna get rid of this problem."

It took a few seconds for what he was saying to sink in, but then Mom started crying. "No, Matt, don't talk like that. What are you saying?"

"Shut up! Admit it; you don't want me anyways. Well, I'm gonna take care of your problem."

Mom knew what he meant and kept crying. I had no idea.

He turned to me. "Juanito, do me a favor. No matter what happens, I want you to stay here with your mom. I'm gonna go upstairs, and I'm gonna take care of the problem. And when the problem's fixed, don't let anyone go upstairs, okay?"

Mom was now screaming. "No, Matt, don't do this! Don't…no!"

I saw how upset my mom was. "Mom, stop, it's okay." I didn't know what was going on, but it seemed like the thing to say.

Dad got up from his chair and walked upstairs. We kept sitting there. Mom wanted to follow him, but I held her back. I figured whatever was going on, she was better off with us downstairs than up there with him.

All of a sudden I heard a loud *bang!*

Then I understood—*Dad just shot himself!*

I ran upstairs. Strange as it seems, I was concerned about him. I opened the bedroom door and looked in. There was Dad, sprawled on the bed, a shotgun resting on top of him.

He sat up and gave a little laugh. "Heh-heh! I guess you *do* love me!"

Then he shouted loud enough to be heard by the others downstairs, "Okay, I've got one loyal one. The rest of you can go to hell!"

As I stood there in shock, he called to me. "Come here, Buddy." Not knowing what else to do, I sat beside him on the bed. He put his arm around me in a gesture of affection. We shared a surreal moment.

After a few more minutes of just sitting, he told us all to go back to bed.

Nobody said a word about any of this the next day...or ever.

That year, my mom got a job washing dishes at a company down the road from where we lived. She walked to the job along the busy highway we lived on, about a five-mile round trip. As fall turned to winter, she continued walking, in the snow on a highway with no sidewalks, to get to work. (Can I just say, when I overhear people deride Hispanics as "lazy" it drives me crazy—not just about the over-generalization, which is meaningless, but also because people like my mom completely disprove such nonsense.)

On one cold, snowy morning about 5 a.m., while it was still dark outside—she remembers clearly it was a Thursday—my mom started her usual trek to work. As she approached the busy highway she slipped off the side of the slightly raised road and fell into the ditch. She lay there for a moment. When she tried to get up, she kept slipping on the steep slope. After she had fallen to the ground several times, she lay on her back, paused again, and looked up into the still-dark morning sky. For some reason, her soul opened up to

God. With childlike innocence, she prayed—not just about getting up from being stuck in the snow, but about trying to get up from being stuck in life.

"Hello?" (How else would you start a conversation with a Being you can't see or hear?) "Hello, my name is Norma. And we need help. I don't know if You are real. Please help us."

She finally managed to drag herself out of the ditch and finished her walk to work. Twelve hours later, she turned around and came home. As she frequently did, she had squirreled away some discarded food from plates she was about to wash and brought it home in a trash bag. This was often all she had to give to us for supper at night, thanks to my dad drinking and gambling away all our money.

That weekend, we were all gathered in the kitchen. As she often did on cold days, Mom opened the stove and lit it. Then we closed all the doors into the kitchen so it would get warm. My dad didn't want to heat the whole house so this was a common practice on weekends when everybody was home. As pathetic as that might sound, those family gatherings in the kitchen on winter days are actually some of my favorite childhood memories. We bundled up and actually felt warm. We sang songs, and Mom told us stories that made us laugh. I can still remember her reading *Peter Rabbit*. Of course, she couldn't read a word of English. As she opened each page and showed us the pictures, she would make up the story on the spot. Each time she "read" it, the story would change. But we didn't mind. Those truly precious moments showed me how a family could be—how love and warmth could flow without measure and how care and kindness and humor can make unbearable circumstances tolerable.

On this particular day, we heard a knock at the door. That was weird, because nobody came to our house uninvited (and few were ever invited). Ours wasn't a typical house in a typical subdivision. If anyone knocked on our door, they had made a determined effort to get there for a specific reason.

My first thought was that someone was coming after my dad. But Dad wasn't at home. He hadn't come back the night before (he was probably passed out on a friend's couch or hooking up with some woman in her apartment).

My mom said, "Juanito, go see who that is."

I went out to the living room, and opened the door. A kindly American woman, who spoke to me in Spanish, said, "Hi, my name is Grace Walters, and the Lord Jesus Christ has sent me to help you."

I had no idea who Jesus Christ was—my church experience with my grandparents was long forgotten. So I turned to call out to my mom.

"Hey Mom, there's a lady here who knows some guy named Hey-soos!"

There were a lot of guys with the name "Jesus" in the Latino community, so I wasn't sure which one this woman was talking about.

My mom got up and came to the door.

Grace repeated herself, in Spanish. "Hi, I'm Grace Walters. I'm from Wheaton Bible Church, and the Lord Jesus Christ sent me to help you."

My mom gasped and collapsed on the floor, weeping. She knew which Jesus Grace meant. She knew that God had heard her prayer back there in the snowy ditch. And he had sent one of his angels to help us.

Chapter 10

New Life

Over the coming days and weeks, we got to know Grace, and she got to know us. She had heard about my family from a social worker at Turner Elementary. She and the whole Wheaton Bible Church family welcomed us. When she saw the conditions we lived in, she found us a better place to live. We moved into one of the rent homes they owned on their street, a home where there was food in the cupboards and we all got some clean clothes. I remember there was a bathroom *with a shower!* That was a big deal—actually taking a shower in our own home. The first time I turned on the water, I stood there amazed. I couldn't believe how wonderful that was. They told us that we could shower—actually, that we *should* shower—every day. Really? What about all that water? What if it runs out? I could hardly comprehend that people lived like this.

Members of the church helped find my mom a better-paying job washing dishes at Wheaton College. When they found out my dad had some skills, they helped him get a job as a welder. I remember seeing my dad in a suit, looking respectable. It was a very different picture of him.

We also started going to church regularly. I didn't know much about Christianity up to that point. I had only attended church a few years when I was a little boy in Mexico. I could recall only big, imposing buildings decorated with ornate statues, paintings and gilding. But somehow, I'd missed the part about Christianity linked to a man in history named Jesus who had come from God. So when Grace first told us we could meet Jesus at church, we thought we were actually going to shake hands with a physical person. When we got there, we met the pastor. I thought for sure he was Jesus. But they let me know that, no, he wasn't Jesus. *Well, where is he? Is he in the building somewhere?* I was so naive about religion. But we wanted to thank this Jesus who—we were told—had provided all our food and clothes and a new, clean place to live.

Someone invited me to the youth group. I remember feeling terrified at the thought of walking into a gym, not knowing anybody. A few people said "Hello," but overall I just stood off to the side. I had no idea what was going on. A few students performed a little skit, and somebody gave a message. It was confusing. But there were pretty girls there! As a young man just beginning to feel the stirrings of puberty, I felt both excited and intimidated, but I kept to myself.

The apartment we lived in was only a few blocks from Franklin Junior High, the new school I attended that fall.

Right about then, I became aware of fashion—or rather, my lack of it. Up to this time, all I wanted was clean clothes, anything to make me more like the other kids. We now had many sets of clothes (that had been donated to the church first, then to us). But nothing matched. So while I thought I was cool now and fit in because my clothes weren't stained or threadbare, kids still gawked at my brothers and me. And I thought, *Wait…why the weird looks and side comments? These clothes are clean and don't have holes. We don't smell anymore; we use soap. What gives?* I couldn't figure it out. No one told me how some color combinations work better together than others or how to coordinate prints and solids. My mom didn't know how to put together matching sets of clothes, either. Dressed poorly herself, she was little help.

Eventually, my brothers Tony and Louie caught on to what was acceptable and advised me. "Don't wear those, Juan. They don't go together." I started to learn what to wear and not wear. We then tutored my poor mom, who was also clueless about American fashion.

One day, I got a flyer about a youth camp up at Phantom Ranch in Wisconsin. I was interested, so I told my mom we should go. Then it dawned on me; this was just for students—I'd have to go by my self. I was terrified. And my mom wasn't used to sending us kids anywhere without her supervision. Grace Walters and her husband, who now lived across the street and had oriented us to so much else, explained that it would be safe. She promised us that there would be adults from the church to watch over us. Fear still gripped me.

I eventually conquered my fear and went to camp. I sat in the front row during the programs, where I thought I'd be safe. People were somewhat nice to me, but overall it was awkward. I started pouting and even became hostile. I felt alienated from the other boys in my cabin. I still didn't fit in, but I didn't really understand what was going on.

During the first few days, mealtimes were the highlight for me. The other kids complained about the food. "Ugh, the food is so terrible here!" I wanted to holler to them all, "Are you kidding? The food is fantastic—and there's so much of it!" They had these jars for lemonade, and you could get as much as you want, any time you want. I'd never experienced such an overflowing abundance.

During the day, we played games, and I was pretty good at kickball. Sports was one place I felt like I had some skill, and kids recognized I had ability and picked me to be on their team—despite my looking and sounding different. At night, the camp held programs with singing and a message. I watched with interest, but I still kept at a distance from everything and everyone.

Then came Friday night. They had us meet by a campfire and did the program there. I don't remember the details, but the short skit really moved me. I wasn't one to cry—not in front of anyone. But something stirred inside me. The speaker was my church's youth pastor, Tim Geoffrion. In his message, he talked about Jesus dying, and about how his blood could save me. This was very confusing. He then told an analogy to explain the kind of love Jesus had when he died for us. It was a story about a brave little boy who wanted to help a friend. (I've heard many versions of this same story over the years, but this is the version he told.) It was during war, and some children were playing when a bomb went off. The younger boy was unhurt, but his older friend was taken to the hospital. They both rode in the ambulance. When they got to the hospital, the older boy had lost a lot of blood, so they needed to do a transfusion. This being a military hospital in a war zone, it was not easy to get a supply of blood. But it turned out the younger friend's blood was a match, so through a translator they asked him if he would give blood to save his friend. The boy was not familiar with modern medicine with its needles and tubes, and felt scared. But trying to be brave, he said he would do it. As they laid him on the table and started the transfusion, the little boy had a question. The nurse asked for the translator to come back. Then the boy asked, "Will it hurt when I die?" He thought that giving his blood would kill him! Yet he was willing to do it for the sake of his friend.

I could hardly contain my reaction. Such sacrificial love! And Tim said that's the kind of love Jesus had for me. He would do that—die for me. And in fact, he *did* do that on the cross 2000 years ago. He gave *all* his blood for me. I had never understood the role of Jesus in the Christian message, but this hit home. Then he added: the only thing Jesus wants in return is for you to give your life back to him. And I thought, "I don't have a life. I don't have anything to give him. Why would he want my life?"

Back in my cabin later that night, Tim stopped in to talk with us. He kindly challenged me: "Juan, if you don't know Jesus yet but you want to give your life to him, you can do that right now."

I was self-conscious, but the need in my heart overcame my fear. "I'm ready. I want to do that."

Tim led me in a simple prayer of surrender and acceptance. As best I knew how, I gave my life to Jesus. I knew there was nothing I could do to earn his love and acknowledged that he loved me just as I was. I invited him to forgive me and lead me for the rest of my life—and on into eternity. Tim encouraged me to tell the other boys in the cabin, and they were all very excited for me. The next night, I also told all the campers what I had done. Almost everyone there came up and hugged and touched me. Such a powerful moment! I'd never experienced anything like it in my twelve years on earth. As little as I understood, I understood enough to know I was loved. And I was lovable. God's love was the proof.

Chapter 11

Mad Dad

WHEN I RETURNED HOME FROM CAMP, I got even more involved in church youth group. I wanted to attend anything and everything they had for kids my age—not only because of my interest in Jesus, but also because the environment was now much more accepting and supportive. I still felt a bit like an outsider, but the kids there at least tried to include me.

To my amazement, my dad went through changes as well. With the new clothes we all had, he dressed more smartly. Men didn't always dress up to attend church, but Dad seemed to enjoy looking his best, and he showed up every Sunday in a suit and tie. He began reading the Bible on his own, actually memorizing passages that were meaningful to him. He seemed so sincere. He cut back drastically on his drinking—sober, he was truly a smart man. He'd been a good student when he was a boy, so now his "better angel" seemed to show up in our new settings. He was making decent money as a welder, and we were living a respectable life.

"You like football, Son?" The coach smiled as he walked over to me. Middle school football coaches have an eagle eye for big kids, and my huge frame was easy to spot as I stood by the fence watching the team practice after school on the first day of seventh grade.

"Oh yeah. A lot." Although I was shy, I couldn't hide my excitement at his interest in me.

"Do you play?"

"Yes!"

"Why don't you try out for the team? You attend here, right?"

"Yes. Sure. What do I have to do?"

"Nothing, really. We need more big guys like you. Just go to the locker room, I'll ask one of the managers to get you fitted with some gear."

I had played football in sixth grade with the Rec team, and although I didn't understand the intricacies of the game, I was big, I had drive, and I wanted to be included. So I joined the team that very first day of seventh grade. I played offensive line, a perfect position for someone not that experienced. There was just one rule: "Protect the quarterback!" That I understood! The coaches were really nice; and they were patient with me as I got up to speed. My mom and dad both seemed happy that I was getting more involved in student life. Although dad still occasionally got drunk, I didn't even mind it that much, because it wasn't every day like it had been. Still, football meant I didn't have to be at home as much, which was just fine with me.

In the classroom, because I was so far behind with my minimal language skills, I spent most of my day in special reading classes. Other students would come and go, meaning my days were a series of small classes—with only six or seven other students at a time. This gave me an opportunity to actually get to know some kids. That setting was much less threatening than the large classrooms where I had typically been marginalized and made to sit apart from everyone. I was smart and, with the specialized attention and some remedial work, I was beginning to make sense of the various school subjects everyone else seemed to know so much about already.

When the football season ended, I wanted to find another sport. I tried out for basketball, but I wasn't very good at it; my size worked against me. When spring came around and I found out there was a sport called "track" where all you had to do was run, I figured I could do *that*.

I joined the team, and they put me on the mile, which I think is where they put all the kids they have no idea what else to do with. I joined the team late, so the very next day we were scheduled to participate in a meet. I got on the bus, we drove to the other school, and I sat with all the other kids in the bleachers waiting for my name to be called. I really didn't know how it all worked, but I was too scared to ask anyone. Finally, some of the boys who knew me said, "Hey Juan, this is your event!"

I lined up with the other boys on the white starting line of the quarter mile track. I noticed that they were all stretching, which I didn't really understand, so I just started copying their moves, not even knowing what I was doing. I'm sure I looked ridiculous. Then the gun went off. I clumsily bolted out as fast as I could. To my amazement, not only did I catch up with the other guys, I passed them. *Look at me! I'm winning!* I thought to myself.

By the time the first lap was over, I was really feeling winded. Now I knew why nobody else tried to catch me—in a mile race, you have to pace yourself. By the time we were halfway through the second of the four laps, everybody had caught up. There was only one other kid as slow as me. We ran side by side for almost the whole next lap.

For some reason, everybody was cheering as we came by the bleachers. I realized later that this was a special needs' kid, and all they wanted for him was to beat at least one guy. By the time the fourth lap started, I fell behind even him. As that final lap came to a close, people came running out of the stands to congratulate him; I had to fight my way through the crowd to waddle over the finish line. I was humiliated. The spontaneous name-calling that came my way from teammates for losing to a mentally-challenged boy really hurt. I was so embarrassed that I quit the team the next day.

I started questioning my abilities all over again, and some of the gains from the acceptance I'd experienced earlier in the year evaporated. I went back into my shell—so much so that next year in eighth grade, the coaches had to seek me out to join the football team. I was too unsure of myself to go out on my own.

I had learned one thing that kept me from completely regressing. During this time, I became great at mimicking people. I had learned to be a keen observer of human behavior—both from needing to do that to survive and from not being able to communicate, which left me in the observer role in most settings. What is counter-intuitive about this is that for most people, comparison is a killer. It creates so much unhappiness. Anybody in the mental health profession will tell you that people who are constantly comparing themselves to others are generally miserable. They have to learn to stop doing that to be happy. But for me, comparison worked to my benefit. I learned so much about others and copied them. And that ability made kids laugh. When I copied somebody behind their back, everybody else around me was in stitches. When I mimicked a teacher, those around me screamed in delight. I got into trouble, but hey—after a visit to the principal's office, the kids would later high-five me and think I was cool. Lots of comedians actually make a living doing impressions of famous people; now I had learned that skill. I was starting to become popular because I had developed a reputation for being funny. In truth, it was a persona I put on—the real me, with all my feelings, was hiding behind the clown mask. But this was way better than being teased and spit on.

Although my dad had shown promise in the early years after he started attending church, by my eighth grade year, he began to live two lives. When I got to high school, the drinking started up again in earnest. He still went to church all dressed up, but he was argumentative, and people just didn't want to be around him. He would be disruptive in prayer meetings, and he had a pattern of asking for money from the church leadership (and other well-meaning people he came across). The elders were losing patience, and we eventually were asked to leave the house that the church was providing.

I begged my mom for us to find a place in the town we lived in and not move far. I had friends now, and despite what dad was doing, we liked our church. But in our financial condition, we had a hard time finding a place to live. We finally got accepted at a place with no deposit and no credit check, but you can imagine what kind of a neighborhood catered to people like us. We lasted there barely a year. It was awful.

Around this time, Dad decided one night to take us three boys downtown to visit with some "friends." We got to their apartment in a very seedy part of town. As we sat on the couch, Dad and the three other men started drinking. And drinking. We kids eventually fell asleep on the couch.

Suddenly we were awakened as a fight broke out. "Come on kids! Let's get out of here. Go get in the car." We sped off, but dad was so drunk, he didn't realize where he was or how to get home. He turned down what he thought was the way to get on to the Eisenhower expressway.

"Dad! You're going down an exit ramp! This is the wrong way!"

A car was coming up the ramp and passed us, horn blaring. Dad still didn't get it.

"Look, the cars are coming at us!"

Dad rolled down his window. "Get off the road, losers! Don't you know how to drive?"

"*You're* on the wrong side of the road—turn around!" Fortunately it was so late, there were not many cars. Dad did a hard swerve and ended up spinning completely around, then came to a stop. It's a miracle no one hit us. The three of us boys started crying.

"Will you boys shut up? I can't think. I need to figure out where we are."

In his drunken haze, Dad finally figured out our location—and that we were facing the right direction. He put the car back into gear and started driving. How he found his way home I'll never know. Like so many other times when we should have been dead, by the grace of God we somehow survived a life-threatening mess created by my dad.

I have several memories of being in the car with dad, him driving drunk, and very dangerous things happening. One time he decided to race a stranger next to us when we were almost home. He was probably going 100 miles-an-hour, and then foolishly thought he could take the turn onto our property. As he turned the car at that high speed, it actually flipped, and the car rolled completely over. None of us were wearing seat belts. We went completely upside down before the car landed back upright. Miraculously, no one was seriously hurt, and we were able to drive away. Other times, when somebody had done him wrong, he would drive by that guy's parked car and make us kids shoot his guns out the window at it to "teach him a lesson"! We'd hit the tires, windows, and doors and then drive off before we got caught. At least he had enough control not to make us shoot at people. But come on—kids shooting guns is still crazy and life-threatening! What dad in his right mind would think that's okay?

He'd also pull up to cars with pretty girls and try to flirt with them.

Sometimes, the man in the car would see what he was doing and roll down his window to yell at my dad. "Hey Buddy! What are you looking at?"

"I'm looking at your girl, *ese!* You got a problem with that?"

"Yeah, you're making us both uncomfortable. Stop it."

I tried to calm things down. "Please, Sir, don't argue with my dad! I'm so sorry."

"Shut up, Juanito!" He slapped me on the head.

Then he turned back to the man. "You feel uncomfortable? I'll show you uncomfortable!" Then he pulled out his gun. "Maybe she'd like to be with a real man, eh *chica bonita?* You get in the car with me, I'll show you a real good time!"

Dad's affairs and lack of appropriate sexual boundaries were no secret to any of us. One time, a group of cheerleaders were at my house, and Dad came out of the bedroom wearing nothing but skimpy shorts and no underwear, essentially exposing himself. Disgusted, the girls left the house. He also had a stash of pornography for as long as I can remember and didn't seem to care if any of us kids looked at it. The pile of misery my dad inflicted on people he should have loved and protected was truly astounding.

All my childhood, I never understood why people celebrated Father's Day.

Chapter 12

Popular

I FLOURISHED DURING MY JUNIOR AND SENIOR YEARS of high school. The language barrier was finally gone, and I began getting pretty good grades. I was funny; and to my surprise, I was also becoming popular. I was a recognized athlete. I got even more involved in a thriving Christian youth ministry, Salt Company. I was a team leader, and we had over 1,000 kids from eight high schools coming every week to our events.

My dad was another story. He got drunk more often, and the few times he came to my football games, he made a scene. Coaches dreaded seeing him, afraid of his temper. He never flashed his gun, but with his threats and boasting, everyone was pretty sure he had one. Quite literally, people feared for their lives around him.

Despite the ongoing disappointments from Dad, there was another bright spot during that era. God brought several godly men into my life, men who intentionally helped build a foundation for me. They challenged me but also encouraged me; they simply showed up. They came to my football games, visited me at home, told me I was better than what I thought I was. They helped me find work and fill out paperwork. They believed in me, loved me, and challenged me to believe in myself.

For example, Keith Cody, my best friend in high school, played football with me. He would help me to get up in the mornings for

Bible study and to take me to school. I slept in the garage, and Cody would open the overhead garage door to wake me up, even during winter.

I had never been fathered well, but being mentored really made a difference. A youth pastor named John Henderson made an especially marked impact. We called him "Hendo." He did things for me that a good dad would do. He showed up at my baseball and football games to support me (and was *sober*...that was different!). I played B-level baseball and our games were at 7 a.m. on Saturday. Nobody came to those games, but Hendo was there every week, cheering me on wearing a silly raccoon hat. I could always pick him out even in a crowd, which I think was his point: he wanted me to know he was there. He came to football games and basketball games, even to my house. A lot of people were afraid of my dad, but he wasn't. He got to know my environment and even reached out to my dad.

On one such visit, Hendo had a frank conversation. "I know you have problems, Mr. Ortiz, but you can't take them out on your son. That's not what a good dad does." Hendo was firm but respectful, as he confronted my dad.

"Oh yeah? Well, who are you to tell me what I can and can't do?" Classic defensive Dad.

"This is about what is *right*—not what I want. It's not okay to hit your kids."

My dad got the icy fire in his eyes I'd seen so many times before when he was fuming with anger, coiling up like a snake ready to strike. After his temporary foray into the Christian faith, Dad was his old awful self again— explosive anger, excessive drinking, drug dealing on the side. So in that moment, Dad did what Dad usually did—he picked a fight. He lunged at Hendo, hitting him square in the jaw.

Hendo is the only person outside my family who actually took a punch for me!

Hendo didn't retaliate; he just left the house. Despite that incident, he continued to meet with me and build into me. He repeatedly told me he was "with me" and "for me," that I was "amazing and talented." What Mr. Lowery did for me in grade school, Hendo was doing for me in high school.

And Hendo wasn't the only mentor in my life. Tim Geoffrion, the youth leader who had led me to Christ at camp, continued to encourage and mentor me. One of my football coaches, Jim Rexillias, was also a strong male role model and example for me. He lived with conviction and compassion—a blend I'd rarely seen in one man.

I had these great mentors now, and I was popular and good at sports. In so many ways, my life was coming together. But though my life had improved, my dad continued to lurk in the shadows. He was now one of the biggest drug dealers in my school. He sold pot to kids I knew. What a bizarre contradiction! On any given day, some students would talk to me about spiritual things, and other students would ask me how they could score some weed from Dad.

I was chosen as Homecoming King my senior year. It blew me away to think about how different my life was from just a few years earlier. I'd come a long way from sitting in that desk off by myself, being teased and spit on.

That Christmas, a group of students from Salt Company held a Christmas party. My friends surprised me with a varsity jacket that had my letters sewn on it. They made a big deal of stopping the party, calling me up front, and saying they had this special gift for me. I was joking around like I always did, but when I opened the box and saw what it was, I was speechless. I couldn't afford that jacket—even though all my buddies had one—but I was so overcome with emotion, I had to walk out of the room. To feel the acceptance of all my friends when years earlier I had been the outsider touched me deep inside.

Crazy stuff was still happening to me because of my dad. On the night we played our Homecoming game, Dad came to the field drunk. I was on the track being recognized as the Homecoming King, and up in the stands, I saw my dad get into a fistfight. He got arrested and was led out in handcuffs. So many people knew that out-of-control drunk was my dad—a fact he shouted as he was led away. I was humiliated.

Dad's drug dealing affected me too. One time, sitting in the front hallway at school, a couple of burnouts came up to me.

"Hey Juan!"

"What's up?"

"Where's your dad at?"

"I don't know. Why do you want my dad?" I knew, of course.

"Come on! (Wink, wink!) Where can we get a hold of him?"

I got mad and walked away. *No matter how much I try to make my life better, I can never get away from this guy! Even at school when he's nowhere around, he's making my life suck!*

A few kids started spreading a rumor that I was doing drugs. Some teachers and administrators, who knew about Dad's reputation, thought the same. One Christian friend confronted me, pushing me up against a locker.

"How can you be smoking weed and selling that stuff? You're a Christian and a leader!"

"I'm not doing that!" I pleaded with my eyes and voice.

He stayed in my face. "I think you're a liar, and it's disgusting! You're a hypocrite!"

Though had Dad offered to smoke with me, I steadfastly refused. People thought I had problems I *didn't* have—and I hid the problems I *did* have! At home, I continued to intervene when Dad got drunk and beat up Mom. There was no support from my family, no concern for my grades or helping me with my schoolwork. I had to face every challenge, ever difficulty, and every milestone without their input.

One of the teachers called me into her office and accused me of being a problem kid. "You are a disgrace! I'm so tired of your lack of respect for the school and for teachers!"

As a Christian, I knew I shouldn't be combative, even when falsely accused. So I didn't mouth off, I just listened.

She continued. "You are so close to failing, Juan. You're over your limit of days you've missed school. I'm telling you, if you miss—or are late one more day—you're not going to graduate. You got that?"

I dropped my head to my chest. *You have no idea what is happening in my life and what I'm going through. And it's clear to me you don't really care. You've got your mind made up without even knowing. Why won't you try to understand me?*

She never asked why I was late or why I missed school. I didn't feel safe enough to tell her, but it still would have helped to know she was trying to enter my world to get some answers.

Defeated, the last bit of air expired from my almost empty self-esteem balloon. "What do you want me to do, Ma'am? I get it— I'm a loser. I'm not going to make it. You might as well fail me now."

She stared at me for a moment, her eyes squinting. "You know, you remind me of a kid I counseled at another school here in the Chicago area. His name was John Belushi. He was a total loser, too."

Now she was comparing me to an actor who died from a drug overdose.

I went home dejected. As usual, Dad came home late, drunk, and started beating my mom. My brother and I were big enough to pull him off. We got out of bed and threw him out the front door. Then I lay down on the couch. I ended up sleeping there the whole night without any more interruptions.

I woke up at 10 a.m. the next morning.

Late again.

I went to the bathroom, and I just started to cry. I hid my tears when anybody could see me, but in the bathroom, I could let them flow.

I am a loser, I told myself. *Now I'm not going to graduate. I'm so embarrassed.*

All of a sudden I heard someone yanking on the door handle, trying to force his way in.

"What?"

"Who's in there?" My dad's voice outside the door.

"It's me, Juan. What do you want?"

He could hear my muffled crying. "What's wrong?"

"Nothing, Dad. I'm just going to the bathroom. Leave me alone."

"Open the door!"

"Dad, I'm going to the bathroom!"

"No you're not; something is wrong. Open the door." He pulled on the door, and the flimsy hook broke. He saw me wiping away tears.

I got up to leave.

"Where are you going?"

"Nowhere, Dad. Just leave me alone!"

"What's going on?"

"What do you care anyway?"

We went back and forth like that for a few minutes.

He finally pushed me down so I was sitting on the toilet lid. He sat down across from me on the edge of the tub. His voice changed from the earlier harsh tone. "What's wrong? Tell me. I want to know." There was a softness to him now. He repeated himself, almost sounding fatherly. "I want to know."

"Alright. Here's the deal: I'm not going to graduate. I'm gonna get suspended."

"Why? What did you do wrong? You're a good kid. You're Homecoming King. You're like the best kid there."

"Dad, I've missed too many days of school. I'm a loser. I'm a failure. I'm not gonna make it."

There was a pause. I had no idea what would come out of my dad's mouth next. "Why don't you tell them the truth?"

"What do you mean?"

He looked down at the floor. "Why don't you tell them that your *dad* is a loser. That he's a drunk and hits you. That he shows you dirty magazines and screws other women. Tell them I'm the reason for all the bad stuff that's happening—not you."

What was this? My dad confessing his sins? Owning the damage he's done? Admitting the mess he's made of his life—and mine? I was speechless.

And in the silence, a hairline crack crawled across the wall of my hardened heart. A tiny fracture allowed a momentary flash of love for my dad, as weird as that sounds.

Then he hugged me, kissed me, and told me he loved me.

I said nothing. I got up and decided I had to face my fate. I prayed. *God help me. I can't do anything about this. It's all in your hands.*

I finished getting dressed and walked to school. When I got there, nobody said anything about me being late. I do not know why, nor did I ask.

That day, I did not get suspended.

That spring, I graduated from high school.

That summer, Dad got arrested and went to prison.

Chapter 13

College Life

"WHY AREN'T YOU GOING TO COLLEGE, JUAN?"

My youth pastor, Tim, who had made such an impact on me at camp, was surprised to hear about my post-high school plans.

"I've got a job now—two jobs, actually. I'm just going to keep working; my parents need the money."

My employment the summer after high school was a part-time job in the kitchen at Wheaton College and another part-time job at a U-Haul rental store.

"College would really benefit you, Juan."

"I'm not a smart person. I wouldn't do well at college."

"What are you talking about? You're very smart!"

Yeah, sure, I thought to myself. *That's what you tell every kid. You're a youth pastor. That's the kind of thing you're supposed to say.* "Well, I don't really know how it works. How do you even sign up for college? Where would I go?"

"That's not the hard part. You have to make up your mind. Once you decide to go, I can help you figure out the rest."

And so, with Tim's help filling out the forms, I signed up to attend Trinity College in Deerfield, Illinois.

Two weeks later, my father got arrested for domestic abuse.

Mom and Dad had another one of their fights. He pounded her down into a whimpering pile and stood over her victoriously. Shouting threats, he stormed out and drove off leaving mom on the floor, slumped against the wall, barely conscious. Just a few minutes later there was a knock at the door, and a concerned woman's voice spoke from outside. "Norma? Are you okay? I heard screaming."

I opened the door. There stood our neighbor, Julie. She saw my mom on the floor and ran to her.

"Oh, my God! What happened? Are you okay?"

"*Mi esposo.* He…" Mom stopped herself.

"Matt did this to you?" she asked.

Mom nodded.

"Does he hit you all the time?"

"*Si.*"

"That's it. We're calling the police."

My mom just sat there—unwilling to actively agree but unwilling to disagree.

In a few minutes, the police arrived and got the story.

"Mrs. Ortiz, here's the thing. If you press charges, we'll arrest him the minute he sets foot on the property. But we need to know this is what you want to do."

Julie chimed in. "You have to do this, Norma!"

Then I spoke. "Mom, if ever there was a time to have Dad arrested, this is that time."

Mom looked so conflicted. I knew she was scared and angry and sad. She was afraid of what Dad would do. And she was afraid of being alone. Of being broke. How would she make it on her own with six kids? (My youngest brother, Gabe, was a baby at the time.)

Yet she couldn't bear the thought of more pain. Dad had to be held accountable. She agreed to work with the police.

The police parked in the neighborhood but not right in front of the house. A while later, my dad pulled into the driveway. As soon as he got out of the car, several squad cars appeared, lights flashing, and officers swarmed him. Dad started swinging, and they forced him to the ground, handcuffing him. I saw the whole thing as I stood at the big picture window at the front of the house. They picked him up off the ground and escorted him to the squad car. Just then, he caught my eye and glared. He said nothing, but I got the message loud and clear. *You did this to me! I'm gonna kill you!*

I walked out on the porch and watched as the police drove off with my dad.

All this happened two weeks before I was to go to college.

Mom approached me, panic in her eyes. "Juan, you can't leave me now. How am I going to make it? You can't go to college."

"I know, Mom. Don't worry. I'm not going to go anywhere. I'll take care of you."

Tim and the other youth leaders heard about what happened. They strongly encouraged me to stick to my original plans and go to college.

"No way. I can't leave my mom."

"She'll be fine, Juan. You have to think about yourself and your future."

Confused and conflicted. I finally came up with a plan. "Mom, I've decided that I'm going to go to college. I'll get an education, and then I can get a good job. I'll come back home and live with you for the rest of my life." I was serious about that. For me, there would be no wife, no kids. I would give back to my mom for all she'd given to me.

Through her tears, Mom hugged me like she would never let me go.

The weekend of freshman orientation, I tossed my small duffel bag in my blue Chevy Impala—I'd stenciled "Trans Am" on the trunk—and arrived at Trinity College. After finding my dorm room, my mom and I went in and sat on my bed. Mom cried during the whole trip. Now we just sat there while she cried some more.

Without warning, the door burst open and in walked Bob Southworth, my new roommate. He had his whole family with him—mom, dad, sister, brothers. All well-groomed, attractive, outgoing. "Hi! I'm Bob. You must be my roommate."

"I'm Juan, and this is my mom, Mrs. Ortiz."

Suddenly, I felt very Mexican in the presence of this all-American family—like I had on a poncho and sombrero with my donkey tied up outside.

After a brief chat, my mom and I left the room and went to the freshman orientation activities. When it was done, I drove Mom all the way back to Wheaton, both of us crying the whole way. In my mind, I must have quit school five times on that hour drive. In the end, I decided to finish what I started.

My roommate, Bob, was a great guy, but he and I were opposites in every way imaginable. He was organized; I was undisciplined. He kept a rigid schedule; I slept in and missed classes. He was serious; I was a cut-up. Despite our differences, we ended up becoming great friends that year.

Another one of my suite mates was a guy named Kevin Olsen. He and I, along with a great cast of characters I met in the first few days at school, became good friends. They picked up quickly that I was unsure of myself and needed some guidance. They looked out for me that first year, and we became a true band of brothers. Kevin was especially important because he had come from the east coast with a friend, Becky Hopkins. He persuaded her to attend Trinity; and without her, my future would have been very different.

College life was a blast. We stayed up late and talked and laughed…and sometimes even did our homework! Bobby got up early when he had to—and encouraged me to be more disciplined. That was always a struggle for me. Yet my sense of humor helped me become as popular at college as I'd been in high school.

One of the highlights of my college days was playing soccer for Coach Mark Schartner. We are still dear friends—and I still call him "Coach." Coach played such a huge role in my life in a very difficult time of my life. My dad was in prison, I was away from home for the first time. He was like a father to me—a good father. More than anything, he helped me to believe in myself. I had never played soccer, I went out for it because they needed guys. So I had to learn how to play—which was sometimes hard. Coach treated me with kindness, but didn't take it easy on me. He'd tell me, "I believe in you, but you need to believe in yourself. Get up and do something with your life." It was so appropriate for where I was. But he was also the guy who would hug me—and still does whenever he sees me.

In the midst of this wonderful time, there was one significant burden—my parents. My mom called me every day. She was lonely and scared, and I was her main person for support. In addition to her calls, my dad had somehow tracked down my number at school. He called from jail, telling me I needed to help him get an attorney. He threatened to kill my mom once he got out. I suppose it was a sign of my co-dependence, but I actually went to several of his hearings. It's a weird feeling watching your dad get brought into the courtroom in an orange jumpsuit, hands cuffed. He was sentenced to ten years in prison for domestic abuse. He went off to prison, and I was actually relieved I wouldn't have to deal with him and comforted knowing he could no longer pound on my mom.

On top of being busy with school, I worked three jobs to make money to help pay bills for my mom. I went home every weekend so my mom wouldn't have to be alone. I also visited my dad once a month in the Joliet prison. Why I did that I don't even know. All he did was yell at me. "You better get me an attorney. I'm gonna kill your mom for this. And send me some money, too!"

"Yeah, Dad, whatever. I gotta go now." Each time I went, it was the same story. And each visit, I couldn't wait to get out of there.

Kevin's friend Becky became popular with my suite mates. She was really attractive, and I remember thinking, *I know I'll never get married, but if I ever did, I would want a girl like that.* Which is what every other guy I knew thought, too! One night, Kevin asked me to go study with a group of friends at the Denny's restaurant near campus. I didn't have any money, but he offered to pay, so I went along. Becky was among the seven or eight students who ended up going. As we sat around, I entertained everyone with some of my funny stories. In one of them about football, I mentioned playing for Wheaton North.

"Wheaton?!" Becky interrupted.

Her high voice and over-stressing the "e" in Wheaton sounded like a mouse squeak. I could hardly keep from laughing.

"I know people in Wheaton. Who do you know there?"

Trying not to sound rude, I said, "I'm kinda in the middle of a story here. Can we talk about this later?"

She apologized for interrupting. But after our study time was over, she took me aside. "So who do you know in Wheaton?"

"Lots of people. I grew up there. I went to Wheaton Bible Church."

"Wheaton Bible Church?! Do you know Herb and Claire Wolf?"

"Oh yeah, I know them well."

"They're my aunt and uncle!"

"Wow. They're great. They've been incredible to me."

Then I remembered a conversation they had with me a week before I started college. They said, "Juan, our niece is coming from the east coast this weekend to attend Trinity. She knows only one other person there. Would you be willing to have dinner with us and meet her?"

I declined the invitation because I had so much else to do. But it was Becky they wanted me to meet. And here it was a couple months later, and I was sitting in a Denny's chatting with her.

Becky was dating a total hunk at the college at that time, a guy we called Tarzan. But despite that, as she and I talked that night, we really hit it off, and a strong friendship began. We often ate lunch together and hung out. She really seemed to care about me. She also sensed there was stuff going on inside me that I wasn't talking about.

Finally at lunch one day, she came right out and asked, "So what's the deal with you? Tell me more about your family." I knew she was trying to get me to open up about the pain I was carrying that was just beneath the surface. But I wasn't ready to talk to anybody about it, let alone this gorgeous girl all my friends were gaga for. It also occurred to me Tarzan would probably kill me if he saw how much time I was spending with his girlfriend. (Then again, I also got beat up a lot growing up, so I wasn't all that scared!)

Becky perceived there was a gap between what she knew about me—my charisma and funny exterior—and the rest of me that I didn't show anyone. She kept pressing, probing for what was the real Juan underneath the jocular exterior.

One Friday, she asked me what I was doing that upcoming weekend.

"Um, well, I'm not going to be around."

"What are you doing?"

"Nothing really, just not being here."

"Juan, tell me. What's happening that you won't be here?"

I didn't want to say I was going home to be with my mother. But I finally relented. "If you must know, I'm going home to visit my mom."

"That's cool. You know, some time I'd like to go with you so I could visit my aunt and uncle."

I kept putting her off, because I was afraid she would want to stop by my apartment, not just get a ride. I didn't want her to see the state of my family. After a while, though, I agreed to take her with me to Wheaton. I insisted I would drop her off and then pick her back up at her aunt and uncle's house. We did that several times. As our friendship deepened, I finally worked up the courage to have her come by for a visit.

When we arrived, she was very gracious. And as we were leaving, my brothers pulled me aside: "Juan, you have got to marry that girl!"

I warned them, "Don't say anything. We're just friends."

Even though Becky had broken things off with Tarzan, our relationship was still just a friendship. We were together a lot, but never as boyfriend and girlfriend. She was one of my most trusted friends, and as she kept probing, I started to disclose bits of my story.

A short time after Becky's first visit to my home, my mom invited Becky and me to come to a fund-raising spaghetti dinner where she'd been hired as one of the cooks. My mom and a handful of other ladies were in the kitchen preparing the food. We both went back to see her, and my mom just gushed over me, showing me off to her fellow cooks.

"This is my son Juan! He is going to college. I am so proud of him. He is going to be a doctor and a lawyer." I still remember she kissed me and got spaghetti sauce on my cheek. "And this is Becky, Juan's girlfriend."

I was embarrassed. My mom had meant to say, "This is Becky, a friend of Juan (who is also a girl)." But in her broken Spanglish, she called Becky my girlfriend. I was worried maybe Becky thought I was calling her my girlfriend behind her back.

As we left the kitchen to go back out to the dining area, I apologized. "I'm so sorry my mom embarrassed you."

"What do you mean?" Becky asked.

"You know, she gets her words mixed up, and she called you my girlfriend. Her English is not very good."

Becky looked right at me. "Well, what's wrong with that?"

And I thought, *Uh, what part are you saying might not be wrong?*

She placed her hands on both hips. "Seriously; what's wrong with us being boyfriend and girlfriend?"

I was stunned. "You want that?"

She had a twinkle in her eye. "I think it would be fun!" And she took my spaghetti-smudged cheeks in her hands and kissed me right there in the hallway.

From that very night, Becky and I started dating. I told my suite mates, and they were dumbfounded. They teased me mercilessly. "How could a guy like you win out over all of us?" But they were genuinely happy for me. Becky and I were together all through college. And just after graduation, she became my wife.

Chapter 14

Unpaid Bills

"YOU OWE HOW MUCH?"

My mom showed me several threatening letters from creditors—a "gift" from dad—even though now he was no longer a part of her life. Among the most strongly-worded documents was a summons to appear downtown in court.

Mom was almost in tears. "It looks like it's a lot. I don't know how much exactly. What am I going to do?"

I stared at the pages spread out on the kitchen table. All their marriage, Dad handled the finances—Mom was completely left in the dark about what they made, what they owed, and where the money went. In the years before his imprisonment, Dad maxed out several credit cards, took out two car loans, and had several big-ticket items on layaway.

Now the creditors were coming after him—but really, coming after Mom. By virtue of marriage, she was legally responsible for his irresponsibility. She had recently been kicked out of her apartment for failing to pay the rent, and was now facing even more humiliation from this strangling debt that she didn't cause and hadn't even known existed.

"Let me handle this, Ma. I'll figure out something."

I had no idea what to do. I was too embarrassed to tell Becky or any of my friends at college. In my ignorance, I figured I would go to court and just see if I could reason with the judge.

I went to a second-hand store and bought a brown corduroy suit. Then I drove to the courthouse in downtown Chicago. I sat there waiting in the courtroom with a lot of other low-income, crying, angry people. I saw several other threadbare corduroy suits, too.

A clerk called out: "Matt Ortiz!"

I raised my hand.

"Approach the bench."

I meekly shuffled forward.

He looked at me over his reading glasses with no emotion. "You're Matt Ortiz?"

"I'm not, Sir."

A moment of dumbfounded surprise. Then an irritated response. "Well, who are you? And where is Matt Ortiz?"

"He's my father. And he's in prison."

"Well, what are you doing here?" Again, not a shred of compassion or understanding. Only frustration.

"Um, well, the letter was sent to my mom."

"Is your mom still married to him?"

"Yes, Sir."

"Well, then she's responsible. Where is she?"

"She doesn't really speak English."

That was only partly true. She probably could have understood enough to interact with the judge. But I was trying to protect her and our family.

"Are you to tell me you're representing your mother and father because they can't be in court?"

"Yes, Sir."

"Do you have an attorney?"

"No, Sir."

"Do you know what the charges are?"

"Uh, well, I'm not sure. I kinda read the letter—"

"You *kinda* read the letter? Look, your dad owes $14,000 (I don't remember the exact amount, but it was way into five figures), and this needs to be paid."

"Fine, I'll pay it."

"How are you gonna pay this?"

"Well, I'm working, and I could give some money."

"How much could you give?"

"I could give $20."

He rolled his eyes and pulled off his glasses. I could tell what he was thinking. *Young kid, second-hand clothes, obviously another low-life, wet-back looking for an easy way out.*

"No, no, Son, you don't understand. We need 50 percent of the debt paid today. You will pay that now."

"I don't have anywhere near that."

"Can you borrow from someone—a relative maybe?"

"No, Sir."

And it went on like this. I don't remember all the details of that day, but I do recall needing to come back multiple times over the next few weeks to face different judges and explain our situation. Looking back on it, I wish my Mom would have just declared bankruptcy and been done with the mess my dad created. These were not her debts. But I had a strong sense of responsibility— and no clue how to handle it or how to get past my shame to ask for help.

At some point, the court finally agreed I could pay small amounts and start chipping away at the debt—along with the hefty finance charges layered on top. Bit by bit each week, I set aside every dime I could spare. This went on throughout my college years. By the time I left school, I had taken out thousands of dollars in student loans. Instead of paying for college, I used that money (along with almost everything else I made) to pay off the liability from Dad's reckless spending.

Mom never knew how I'd taken care of that debt. No one knew. A huge sense of responsibility kept me working at it. Fear and embarrassment kept the secret locked inside me.

My mom filed for divorce while Dad was in prison. Even with their marriage ended, Dad continued his tirades—from prison. He called collect, and if we didn't accept the charges, he threatened us. He went off on huge rants full of threats. He told us he knew a guy who was getting out that week, and that he was sending him to our house to kill us all! Even from prison, he terrified us. And for a long time, we were paralyzed by it.

Of course, the prison officials knew nothing of these conversations. They thought he was a model inmate. In prison, he acted funny and engaging, and even took on a renewed interest in the Bible. After only four years, he was released for good behavior, which we knew was only a pretense. He got out in December 1984, right after I graduated from college.

Dad thought my siblings and I would be glad to see him now that he was free. But nobody cared. Much to his surprise and disappointment, I was the only one of us who even showed up the day he got out. I helped him find a place to live and through a friend's dad, got him a decent job driving a bulldozer. He was incensed that no one else contacted him.

Now that I was out of school, I needed full-time work. My friend Bobby got me a job in the mailroom of an investment-banking firm. My other buddy Hendo said he wanted me to come help him start a church that spring and lead the youth ministry. That was a very exciting prospect for me—I loved kids, and I loved the thought of being able to work in full-time ministry. I told the people in the mailroom I'd be leaving once the church got up and going. Becky and I had set our wedding date for April 27—and the first service of the new church was going to be April 28! I was concerned about how that would work, but Hendo joked that he didn't see a problem—as long as I changed the date of my wedding! The real solution was that I would help plan the launch of the new church, then miss the first few services. As important as the new church was, everyone agreed it would work out fine for us to get married and go on our honeymoon first.

The bigger problem was that since my dad had been released from prison, he had struggled. He couldn't make the adjustment to life on the outside. I'm sure he was depressed, sitting alone in his apartment all the time when he wasn't working. But all he expressed was frustration and anger. He made repeated threats against family members. None of us were interested in pursuing any kind of a relationship with him. Nobody called him. Nobody visited him. Frankly, we were done with him, and we'd moved on.

Dad simmered in rage, angry that the control and fear he used to instill in us no longer worked. Truth is, by that point in our lives, we had come to regard him as mostly pathetic. In his frustration, he got even more boisterous and threatening.

"You kids are so ungrateful! Here's what I'm gonna do. I'm gonna kill Luis. Then I'm gonna send Luis' liver to Gracie. Then I'll kill her, and send her heart to Tony. Then I'll kill Tony and send his stomach to your mom! And then, Juan, I'm gonna come to your wedding and kill her!"

Even though Becky didn't know my dad well, her response to him was classic Becky. "You know what Matias? You're crazy! You're insane! You need to shut up!"

Because we didn't take Dad seriously and because we felt obligated to do so, we invited him to attend our wedding. Looking back on it, I wish we hadn't. I think we were not as assertive—or wise—as we should have been. We should have told him he wasn't welcome. We asked a friend to act as a bodyguard—to watch him and be prepared to respond to any of his antics. And though Dad showed up, we were grateful that he didn't do anything inappropriate—other than mutter under his breath that he was gonna kill mom! With him there, the day could have been a disaster. Much to our delight, our wedding was instead a beautiful celebration that went off without a hitch.

A few months later, my dad was staying at a friend's house where some little girls were having a slumber party. The way he tells the story, he had been drinking earlier and got up in the middle of the night to go to the bathroom. As he walked out through another room, he tripped over one of the little girls lying on the floor. She woke up, but he just stumbled on to the bathroom. Then he returned to his bedroom and thought nothing of it.

The little girl later told her mom, "A man in the house woke me up and was on top of me." The mom notified the authorities, and my dad was arrested. I went to his first court appearance on my birthday and watched as the prosecutor held out my dad's rap sheet. Dad was clearly in trouble, and he knew it. Dressed in an orange jump suit with leg irons and chains, he looked over at me and told me I needed to get him a lawyer. But I did nothing. Later he was tried, and I was there for that process as well. He was convicted of child molestation and sentenced to 25 years in jail. He refused to admit any wrongdoing. Something seemed to shift inside of him, though, and in a strange way, he seemed to show concern for me. Just after he was sentenced, he turned to me and said, "Don't worry about me, Son. You're married now. Just get on with your life." And they took him away.

What surprised me most was what happened next. I went out into the parking lot, sat in my car...*and wept!* I couldn't fathom it. Why wasn't I relieved? With Dad's conviction, at last I'd be done with him (at least for the next 25 years). And he wouldn't be able to threaten or hurt my mom and siblings anymore. Why did I care about him? Why wasn't I happy?

Looking back on it now, I believe I understand what was going inside of me that day. In my heart of hearts, deep down where we all are just a little boy or girl, I wanted a daddy. I wanted to have a father I could be proud of, and to have him be proud of me. I wanted to have a normal family. But instead, I got this crazy man. He'd scared me, abused me, and embarrassed me over and over. Yet the son...the little boy inside...still cried out for Dad to be a dad.

Dad spent the next fourteen years behind bars. I chose to get on with my life. Yet truth be told, the ache in my heart has never completely gone away.

Chapter 15

Full Circle

I MAKE NO SECRET OF THE FACT I struggle with depression; in fact, I have since childhood. Which, considering the chaos of my family, I function well when I am in public, but there have been days when I couldn't even get out of bed. I've had suffocating feelings of inferiority, which show up at unpredictable times and places. I've even been suicidal at times.

None of this has anything to do with how good or bad things are in my life. I have a wife who loves me unconditionally. I have five fantastic children with whom I have a great relationship. I have amazing friends, and many godly, wise and compassionate people who mentor and support me. I have achieved success in virtually every area anyone would think to measure: professional, financial, relational and spiritual.

Yet despite all those circumstances, depression is part of my reality to this day. I remember one particularly dark incident that happened several years ago. I was downtown at Union Station in Chicago, and I felt absolutely hopeless. I was thinking of how to end my life. I walked over to the woman behind the ticket counter. In an almost zombie-like tone, I said, "I'd like a ticket."

"To where?" she muttered mechanically, still looking down.

"I don't know."

Now she looked up at me. "You…don't…know." She repeated my words sarcastically, emphasizing each one with a pause in between. She reminded me of the judges in the courtroom when I went to settle my dad's indebtedness. "Well, sweetie, you have to have a destination."

"I don't have a destination."

"You have to have a destination."

"I want a destination."

She was bewildered, but took it in stride—like this was the third time today she had to deal with a nut case.

"You sit over there, and you make up your mind. Then you come back here, and tell me your destination."

I went over to the bench, which was right near a pay phone. I decided to call my buddy Hendo.

First ring. I told myself, *I am such a loser!*

Second ring. *I just can't succeed.*

Third ring. *My kids and wife deserve better.*

He picked up. "Hello?"

"Hendo, yeah, it's Juan. I figured I ought to tell somebody what's going on. I'm done. I'm at the station, and I'm going to take a train to somewhere no one will find me and just end my life."

There was a short pause. "Well, Juan, I just gotta tell you, no one could blame you. If anyone has the right to do that, it's certainly you."

That was not what I expected to hear.

He went on. "One thing bugs me though."

I took the bait. "Oh yeah? What?"

"It's just that with so many victories on God's side of the equation—so many amazing things that have happened to you despite how bad it's been—it seems so sad the devil is gonna get the last victory."

I was really confused.

"I love you, man. See you later."

And then he hung up.

I'm not suggesting that this is the appropriate thing to say to someone threatening to take his own life. But Hendo knew me well. He knew that having me consider how suicide would let God down in light of all the grace I'd been shown would shock me out of the quagmire of self-pity. He knew I wouldn't go through with it once I saw that ending my life would disappoint God and fill the devil with glee.

I walked back out to the commuter lot where I parked. A voice in my head spoke loud and clear. *That's right! You don't stop until you get home!* I drove back out to the suburbs where I lived. I walked in the door and hugged my wife. I hugged my son. I told Becky what had just happened. "I need to get help."

And with her full support, I did.

God has done amazing things for me over the years. He has done amazing things *through* me, too. But he hasn't completely healed me of the pain inside. To be honest, I don't expect him to (though I know he has the power to do so if he should choose). I believe that I, like all other people in this fallen world, must bear the lasting scars of whatever wounds me. Experiences as a child in my broken family as well as possible chemical imbalances in my brain continue to affect me. God will someday repair all that was broken and restore all that was lost. But that day has not yet come. Likely it will not come until I am in heaven with him.

In the meantime, I do have hope, and joy, and purpose. God is good, and does good for me. The gifts that sustain me are many: my wife Becky, my children, my friends, my mentors, the Holy Spirit inside me who comforts me, the Bible that instructs and guides me, and a continual sense that God is with me and for me no matter what is happening. My moods are not my only reality; they are a part of me but do not define me. True, my on-and-off depression has affected most of my relationships, and my wife has probably paid the biggest price of anyone. But I am able to deal with the effect I have on others as well as myself. I work to rectify any wrong I do and own my responsibility to take care of myself and not blame others. I use the tools I've been given so I can live with my hardships but not be limited by them.

The other struggle I have frequently is that whenever I'm embarrassed, I get angry. I know shame causes some people to slink in the shadows. But when it happens to me, I explode. I don't like it and wish I could change it. I'm sure it goes back to my dad embarrassing us when I was growing up. When it happens now, I feel a hot flash of anger and have to keep myself from hurting those around me. I'm convinced a lot of domestic violence is rooted in these kinds of feelings. It isn't that violent people have too much power. It's just the opposite—they feel powerless. And for me (and many others like me), embarrassment—looking bad or foolish—creates that sense of weakness and shame. In an attempt to compensate for that weakness, I power up, and I lash out.

I write this because while my story is a testimony to God's grace and power, it is not complete yet. God is still at work. My adult years with Becky and our family have been wonderful. I've been a youth pastor, built businesses, become a public speaker, and now combine a great career with freedom to do other worthy projects. I get paid to do many things I enjoy, and yet I do many other things without pay that fulfill me as well. I have a growing avocation that takes me before large audiences to speak about issues like domestic violence, the value of mentors, and the exciting potential for anyone to experience deep, personal change. I tell my story whenever I can—not because I am all that important, but because all the people who loved me and built into me are heroes and can inspire us all. They made me into the man I am today. My story is their story.

My dad served 18 of his 25 years before being deported back to Mexico. He died in 2003. Things never improved between him and me or my other family members. The damage he did to us is his unfortunate legacy.

My mom never remarried, but she has a great relationship with the rest of us. Despite the overwhelming hardships that defined the first half of her life, she never became bitter or resentful. Her sense of humor delights everyone she meets. Her sacrifices for our family are her lasting legacy.

Each of us kids has been on our own journey, and we've worked through the pain from our childhood in a variety of ways. I am grateful for the many good memories I have from growing up together. And despite the trauma we endured, we've found a way to stay connected and be a family of grown-up siblings.

My wife, Becky, and our two sons and three daughters are the absolute delight of my heart. That I have them in my life given the circumstances of my childhood is a daily source of amazement and joy. It would be presumptuous of me to say they are my legacy. In truth, I am theirs. Their transformative love and unconditional acceptance of me—with all my flaws—is beyond anything I ever hoped for or deserved.

In the mid-1990s, my family moved back to West Chicago. Completely unplanned and unforeseen, my kids ended up attending the very grade school I went to over twenty years earlier—Turner Elementary!

One day my son, Steve, who was in third grade at the time, came home excited.

"Dad! In our class, they're talking about drugs. I told my teacher you were a drug addict. She wants you to come speak to the class!"

I called the teacher and tried to explain I was not a drug addict but that Steve was partly right because I did know something about the topic given the family I grew up in. She laughed and was very pleasant. She mentioned they were doing a drug awareness program, and that she would still be honored if I would come to the school and speak to Steve's class. Without thinking much about it, I agreed to come.

I was completely unprepared for what happened when I got there. I hadn't been in the school building since I left as a boy. Though a few things about it had been updated, mostly it was still the same inside as in the early 1970s. I was immediately flooded with memories—some hard, some sad, and some painful. As soon as we walked in the front door, I could see into the office. I saw the counter where my mom and I had stood the first day she walked us to school. I immediately remembered the fear and embarrassment of that day.

We walked down the hallway and arrived at Steve's classroom. The door, the window, everything was unchanged. I had stepped into a time machine, and I was a kid all over again. I don't think I'm exaggerating when I compare it to a PTSD attack. I was barely able to stay in the present and remember how old I was and why I was there.

Fortunately the inside of the classroom had been remodeled, and with my son there, I came back to my senses. When it came my time to speak, I talked for about twenty minutes. When I was done, the classroom erupted with the sound of little hands clapping and the teacher giving me a very appreciative look. Steve left the classroom with me and we walked back to the main entrance of the building. We stood for a moment.

"Dad, that was awesome! You are such a good speaker!"

I was not really expecting such praise from my son. But what he said next undid me.

"I am so *proud* of you. You're the best dad!"

There, right in the lobby, right in front of the office where I'd been humiliated as a boy, I fell on my knees weeping. I hugged Steve and sobbed with joy and appreciation.

The women in the office saw me drop down and came running out.

"Are you okay?"

I looked up at her and my son.

I'd done it. I had broken the cycle of violence that was part of my family. I had instilled in my son the pride in his dad that I'd always wished I could have had for my dad. Steve spoke the words that fathers and sons are supposed to say to each other. Instead of the abusive, manipulative tirades I'd grown up hearing, my son and I were blessing each other.

"Yeah, I'm okay. I really do know it. I'm okay!"

Epilogue

RECENTLY I WAS DRIVING WITH MY BOSS and some clients to Wrigley Field in Chicago. One of them wondered out loud about the outcome of the game we would soon watch. "You think the Cubs will win today?"

"This is Chicago," I quipped. "We're talking about the Cubs. Wrong question!"

Just then, my cell phone rang. "Sorry, let me take this."

My boss and our clients—who are also good friends—started making jokes about the Cubs while I answered my phone.

I picked up. "Hello?"

"Hi. Are you Juan Ortiz?"

"Yes."

"This is Officer Trent Anderson" (not his real name). "I'm from the Glen Ellyn police."

"Is there a problem?" I tried to keep my voice even and steady.

"Nothing's wrong, don't worry. I heard your presentation at the Domestic Violence conference the other day. I just have to tell you, I was really moved by your story. I haven't been able to get it out of my mind."

I breathed a sigh of relief. "Well, thank you. I'm glad you enjoyed it."

The caller paused for just a moment. "I wanted you to know...I found Mr. Lowery."

I was stunned. After I left sixth grade, Mr. Lowery lived only in my memory—though I shared the story of his influence many, many times. I had been so grateful for his kindness during that turning point year, but I'd neither seen nor spoken to him for thirty-five years. It hadn't even occurred to me to try to find him.

I was immediately overwhelmed by emotion. I couldn't say anything. My boss and our clients were busy chatting away. I turned my face toward the car window so they wouldn't see my tears. But my boss picked up on my emotion, and even one of the men in the back seat knew something was going on with me. Their conversation paused, and the car got quiet except for the wind noise from the highway. I still had the phone to my ear.

"Mr. Ortiz? Are you there?"

"Sorry. I'm just...so surprised."

"Well, I just wanted to call to tell you that when I spoke to Mr. Lowery, he remembered you! He would love to see you."

My eyes glistened with tears. I could hardly see the road. "Uh, listen. I'm really sorry. Would it be okay if I called you back? I'm driving right now with some other people. This is a little awkward."

"No problem. Tell you what: I'm going to set up a meeting with Mr. Lowery. And if you don't mind, I'd like you to do me a favor. When I get this all set, will you let me take you to his house?"

"That would be great. Thank you." I hung up the phone.

The Cubs lost the game that day (of course). But I didn't care.

Several days later, as promised, the officer picked me up in an unmarked squad car and drove me to Mr. Lowery's house. When he answered the door, I couldn't believe it—he actually looked the same. A tiny man, horn-rimmed glasses, with the same humongous heart. He gave me a hug.

We sat down, and I started right in. "I know I never said anything back in sixth grade about this, but I am so thankful for everything you did for me. I never responded to you. I gave you no indication of how much joy you were bringing me, yet you kept on loving me unconditionally. I am a transformed man today, and much of it goes back to what you modeled for me. You were the first person outside my family to be truly kind and loving."

As we talked, I was surprised to learn that Mr. Lowery remembered my mom and my dad's names. He recounted all my siblings' names, too. What kind of person can do that?

We had a wonderful lunch together. I cried. Mr. Lowery cried.

The policeman cried.

I have stayed in touch with Mr. Lowery. We've had lunch several times, and even now, he loves to teach me about life. I've spoken all over the country and told the story of Mr. Lowery to thousands of people. The impact of what he did for one little outcast boy continues to reverberate and inspire people everywhere I go. Other than my grandparents' early influence on me and my mom's steady presence, Mr. Lowery was the first ray of light that got into my heart. He brought into my desperate, downcast life the precious gift of hope.

A simple life...unconditional love...thousands and thousands of people touched.

Mr. Lowery since started volunteering in the county jail. He tutors inmates. Through his influence, they're feeling loved and known. They're learning the same thing that he taught me, the same thing my grandparents taught me, the same thing my dear mother taught me, and the same thing a loving church, kind youth leaders, and several mentors taught me throughout my life. It's simply this: love is the most powerful force for change in the world. With love, you can get through any difficulty. With love, you can have new beginnings. With love...

Anything is possible once you accept that you can change.